"Tate's personal history is t
remembered a universal princ
of hope and faith."—C. NORMAN SHEALY, M.D., PH.D., Founder,
American Holistic Medical Assn.

"This book is extraordinary ... a real joy ... documenting
the journey of a sensitive man who could be everyman—his
doubts, his fears, his triumphs are so deeply human and so
universal. It reflects the power of a thoughtful person to draw
on the traditional and the non-traditional approaches to healing and to fashion, from the best of each, a path to
wholeness."—RACHEL NAOMI REMEN, M.D., Medical Director of
the Commonweal Cancer Help Program and a member of the
adjunct faculty of Saybrook Institute.

"Reading this hero's journey was empowering. As a survivor
of a life-threatening illness, I heard the ring of truth throughout Tate's deeply moving story."—LUCIA CAPACCHIONE, Art Therapist and author of *The Well-Being Journal: Drawing On Your Inner
Power to Heal Yourself.*

"A remarkable story. ... It tells how we can share with our
physicians the responsibility for getting well and staying well.
This is a truly inspiring book."—KEN KEYES, JR., author of *Handbook to Higher Consciousness.*

"I know that many people will be inspired and helped by
reading what David Tate has gone through. He has followed
Edgar Cayce's dictum, 'Live something first, then talk about
it.'"—WILLIAM A. MCGAREY, M.D., Co-Director A.R.E. Clinic,
Phoenix, Arizona.

"This is an invaluable book for those dealing with a life-
threatening illness, an antidote to feelings of helplessness and
despair that often accompany a threat to one's survival."—
" :NNETH RING, PH.D., author of *Heading Toward Omega.*

HEALTH, HOPE, AND HEALING

A Survivor of Cancer
and Heart Attack Tells How
He Used Holistic Techniques and
a Spiritual Perspective as Well as
Traditional Medicine in his
Search for Wellness

DAVID A. TATE

M. Evans and Company / New York

Library of Congress Cataloging-in-Publication Data

Tate, David A.
Health, hope, and healing / David A. Tate.
p. cm.
ISBN 0-87131-658-7
1. Tate, David A.—Health.   2. Hodgkin's disease—Patients—United
States—Biography.   3. Hodgkin's disease—Alternative treatment.
4. Coronary heart disease—Alternative treatment.   5. Holistic
medicine.   I. Title.
RC644.T38   1989   89-23833
362.1'9699446'0092—dc20
[B]

First Paperback Edition

M. Evans and Company, Inc.
216 East 49 Street
New York, New York 10017

Design by M. Paul

Manufactured in the United States of America

Acknowledgments

Anyone reading this book will know what an important role my
wife, Judith, has played in my healing and in my life. Since our
marriage, nearly twenty-five years ago, she has been my closest friend
and ally. She initially expressed reservations about my writing this
account of my—of our—lives. Her belief in its value has brought me
great joy.

I want to thank my agent, Oscar Collier, for his confidence in me
as a writer and for his attentive readings of the manuscript, which
resulted in many constructive suggestions. Finally, thanks to George
de Kay, my publisher's president, for his enthusiastic response to the
proposal for the book, for his continued support, and for his editorial
help on the manuscript.

Table of Contents

_____■■■_____

Dedication

This book is dedicated to Dr. James J. Fischer, Dr. Roberta E. Flesh, Dr. Y. C. Siow, and Dr. Robert S. K. Young, master healers and compassionate human beings.

PART I

A Healing Journey

CHAPTER 1

A Healing Journey

Then it happened. *All of the people who I was began to leave me. Parts of me literally and physically, for I could feel my body being diminished, fell away, as if I were a snake shedding its layers of dead skin. Son, gone. Husband, gone. Father, gone. Lawyer, brother, friend, all gone. As these selves peeled away, I descended into an even deeper blackness, spiraling down and down, as if I were on a corkscrew. I was afraid, for I thought I must be dying. When all my selves are gone, what will be felt? What will be left? I wanted to open my eyes, make a sound, paddle toward the shore. I watched the urge die away and momentarily felt at peace. Then terror struck me like a storm. Almost to the bottom! Almost gone! And there will be nothing! Nothing! This agonizing fear lasted but a minute but its white-hot intensity cauterized my soul. I had no more selves to bleed. Gone. Nothing, nothing. I am nothing. Then thought fell away. And I was truly absolutely nothing.*

But—and this is the mystery and the miracle—I did not die. I did not disappear. When I was gone, something else remained. It seems impossible to describe. An awareness, but not an awareness of any thing or any thought, just an awareness. It wasn't thin or ephemeral. The opposite. It was solid and strong and real. It seemed to have no boundaries.

The next thing I knew I was crying. I wept in gratitude and relief. Everything I am was gone, yet I continued to be. At first I had no words for it. And then: I am. I am. And these I did not speak but breathed. When the world stops—all sounds and all sights and all perceptions and finally all thoughts—and you remain to witness it, I tell you it's a miracle.

I paddled the canoe toward shore, rejoicing, first in the holy silence, and then in the words: I am. I am. I am.

I wish to embark on the telling of my story from a place at its center. You will read more about this transcendent experience in its proper context. I placed it here because I think the experience I described lies close to the heart of my healing journey. What began as a narrow search for a cure of a physical disease expanded into a spiritual quest.

Chronologically, my story begins with my first life-threatening illness, Hodgkin's disease, a form of cancer. I describe what happened, what I thought, and what I felt, with as much accuracy and honesty as I am capable of bring to the task of recalling such a painful period of my life. Neither the recollection nor the writing about this part of my life was easy. I suspect it won't be easy to read. Yet I would ask that you allow my words to enter your mind and be felt in your heart; otherwise the significance of my journey into wellness might be diluted. More simply stated, it is important to know where I began if you are to understand the road I traveled.

I wish to emphasize that this is not a how-to book. Rather it is a personal story about my experience in dealing with two life-threatening illnesses, cancer and heart attack. Each person, whatever the circumstances, must find his own path. This is particularly true of people afflicted with a life-threatening disease. Nevertheless, the perspective I've adopted or a particular technique I've employed may resonate within a reader. He or she may think, as I sometimes did when reading a book or an article, "That seems right for me. That is something I must try."

The Importance of Rapid and Accurate Diagnosis: Overcoming Fear

The table of contents will show I pursued a variety of holistic techniques: meditation, Edgar Cayce remedies, acupuncture, psychic healing, and others. These approaches were adjuncts to traditional medicine. Although this is not a story with only one message, there is something I wish to say loudly and clearly: The most important thing you can do when you have a symptom that might be serious is to get an accurate diagnosis. If you are ill, you should receive, as soon as possible, the best treatment Western medicine has to offer, whether it be surgery, radiation, or chemotherapy.

Just a word or two about the first issue, diagnosis. Our natural response when we have a symptom that might be caused by a life-threatening illness is fear. One way of dealing with fear is to deny its existence, to suppress it. The problem with that defense is that it may also lead to a denial of the possible significance of the symptom and, worse, inaction. The only sensible thing to do when faced with the type of symptom I am talking about is to override the fear and call a doctor. In fact, it may be helpful to make an agreement with yourself ahead of time: If the situation ever arises, that is what you will do.

If a diagnosis proves you do have a serious illness, even a possibly life-threatening illness, such as cancer, it's important to realize that your life is not, by any means, over. All cancers are treatable, and depending upon the type and stage, the cure rate can be as high as 100 percent. Still, cancer can and does kill people. A diagnosis of cancer can be scary, even terrifying. But no matter how immobilized you are by the shock of the diagnosis—you will read how deeply it affected me—you must act as expeditiously as possible to commence the treatment suggested by a physician you trust. The choice of treatment is not always clear-cut. If it is not, or you distrust your physician's judgment or competence, you should quickly get a second or even a third opinion. It should never be too much trouble to make sure you are receiving the best medical treatment for your disease.

That is the end of my sermonic message, for that is all I can be certain about—certain in a strict, scientific sense. I believe, strongly, deeply, that a positive attitude significantly enhances one's chances of survival, but I would be hard pressed to prove it. I believe that honesty in acknowledging and expressing emotions—whether pain, rage, anger, or fear—is tremendously important, but I could not prove that either. And the will to live. How I wish I could describe exactly what it means and, better, how to instill it or strengthen it. I believe the will to live has a critical impact on the healing process. My beliefs are based upon my experience. Their validity must be left to each reader. As the title suggests, my story is about more than regaining health. It is about hope, which is both an ingredient in the healing process and a prerequisite for getting us through the day. Hope, no matter how small the measure, is necessary to sustain life. And finally my story is about healing in the broad sense of becoming whole. Wholeness suggests that all of our aspects—our physical, emotional, mental, and spiritual parts—become more vitally engaged and harmonized in the precious process we call Life.

A Case of Emotional and Spiritual Neglect

I don't know which is more neglected in our culture, our emotional selves or our spiritual selves. In my case, before my illness both were shallow and undeveloped. My illness forced me to change. It thrust me on a path of transformation, a slow, arduous journey, still very much in progress. Those abstract questions asked by philosophers and theologians suddenly became pertinent. Who am I really? What is my relationship to other people and what does that relationship demand? Is there a God? What is His nature? What is my relationship to Him and what does *that* relationship ask of me? My search for answers to these questions, and my actions in response to the answers I found, however tentative they were, spiritualized my journey.

For a spiritual quest, it had strange beginnings. Before my illness I had believed in the Judeo-Christian God; I was a believing, church-going Catholic. Not long after I became ill, I lost my faith. I became an agnostic, someone who didn't know, but never someone who didn't care. My conception of God, I believe, was distorted by my needs, some that I was aware of, some not. I knew that if I were to get even a glimpse of the ultimate reality, I needed first to satisfy the ancient dictum "Know thyself." An inner journey can be a narcissistic trip or it can be a means of sharpening perceptions, of removing the cataracts from our inner eye so that we may more clearly see the light.

Increasing Your Chances of Surviving Life-Threatening Illness

The telling of my story, my healing journey, was a journey in itself. For a long time I had wanted to share what happened to me. I wanted to add, for those who were ill or might become ill, to the growing literature of hope. The common theme in the classics in this field—Norman Cousins's *Anatomy of an Illness*, the Simontons' *Getting Well Again*, Herbert Benson's *The Relaxation Response*, Kenneth Pelletier's *Mind as Healer, Mind as Slayer*, Lawrence LeShan's *You Can Fight for Your Life*, and Bernie Siegel's *Love, Medicine & Miracles*, to name a few—is that patients *can* act to significantly increase their chances of surviving life-threatening illnesses. They can act to decrease the chance of becoming ill at all. They may prolong life and add to its quality.

I did not act on my impulse to share how I had responded to my illness. For years I simply thought about what I learned, promising myself that someday I would write it down. Then a time came when I wanted to write and found I couldn't. The reason was simple enough. In order to tell my story fully I would have to return to the past. I would have to descend into the cave where my dark memories slept and awaken them. Looking down at them, with my feet on the earth and my face in the light, seeing them strewn on their coffin-beds of cold rock, was quite enough for me. I turned away. More years passed.

Then in October of 1988 I went to Toronto to participate in the Northeast Psychosynthesis Conference as Hahahanda, an aspirant on the humor path to self-realization who tells his audiences how he met his guru. (Later on I will describe how I became a New Age comic.) At the dinner that preceded my performance several people began talking about life-threatening illness. I joined the conversation and told them a little about my own experience. After dinner, a young woman at our table asked if she could talk with me. She had had a cancerous tumor removed from her brain and was undergoing chemotherapy.

We arranged a time to speak the next day. I told her my story and listened to hers.

Then on November sixth, for no apparent reason, I woke up and went to my typewriter before breakfast—something I've never done—and wrote for several hours. Before the day was through I had written a long summary and a detailed outline of everything I wished to say. I sent the proposal to my agent, and a few days later my publisher submitted an offer.

Was it coincidence, I wonder, that on the day I felt so charged with energy, on the day when my fears and resistance to reexamine my life magically dissolved, on the day I inexplicably decided to tell my story, on that morning of November sixth, the young woman from Toronto was writing me a letter? I don't think so. I think I felt her thoughts, and I think those thoughts affected me. For she wrote to thank me for sharing my story with her. Hearing it, she said, was somehow healing. I like to think that on that morning of November sixth I heard her thoughts with an inner ear and they cured me of my fear.

Illness as a Catalyst
for Making
Deeply Needed Changes

A final thought. Many authors state that illness can be the catalyst for making deeply needed changes that result in a more meaningful and satisfying life. This has been my experience. But surely there are other ways we can learn to grow, to deepen our appreciation of life, to become at times, enthralled with its beauty and sacred mystery. Surely there are other ways to learn. Illness is a path that can lead to inner riches. It is not one I would recommend.

CHAPTER 2

The Diagnosis

C ertain moments in our lives are so traumatic or so beautiful that they are frozen in our minds and can be reproduced like snapshots.

The First Symptoms

The summer sun was hot, especially on the asphalt tennis court. I was leading my brother in the set. Walking back from the net, where I had retrieved a ball, I happened to place my right hand under my left armpit. I felt a lump. My fingers probed. It was the size of a peach pit. Funny, I thought. I put it out of my mind and finished the set. After the set was over, I again felt the lump and, this time, I was worried. What could it be? I told my brother about it and he wagged his head and he said, "It's nothing. Stop being a hypochondriac."

He's right, I thought. I *am* a hypochondriac.

I believed then that the label fit. Ever since I was very young, I had worried excessively about illness and dying. I can't really say why I worried so. Perhaps it was because my father had been in great pain from a leg condition for most of my childhood. Or maybe I absorbed my mother's constant fear that her children would become ill. I had not been a sickly child. But during adolescence I had shot up rapidly and my long frame had never filled out. In one year I had grown nearly a foot to my present six feet, one inch. On the day I first felt the lump, I was twenty-six and weighed 140 pounds. I was not particularly worried about cancer. Naturally I feared the disease when I heard or read about it. But I had no phobia, was not afraid that I might be prone to it. Cancer was a disease that other people got. The prospect of getting it myself was just too horrible a fate to contemplate even for a "hypochondriac."

In the past, I had thought about cancer very little. The poor people who got it were members of a different species, a type of being with whom I could not possible identify. One of my uncles had died from it, but I hadn't been close to him. If I had known someone who had had cancer, I would have probably done my best to avoid the person. It wasn't the fear of catching it so much as the desire to be free from having to be reminded that such a terrible possibility existed. Later on, I understood why an acquaintance who had heard about my condition avoided me. I tried not to blame him.

In my early twenties, my concern was my heart. I monitored it by taking my pulse at various times throughout the day. I often worried when my average of 85 or so beats per minute would inexplicably jump to 125. Once in a while my heart would appear to stop; in reality it would skip a beat or two. Several times I went to see the chief internist at the local hospital, and he always assured me that my heart was just fine. I had become so accustomed to taking my pulse over the years that a strong association between my heart and my watch had formed. One day I placed my fingers on my wrist and glanced down at my watch. For a second a jolt of terror ran through me. I thought that my heart had finally quit. Then I realized what had happened. My watch had stopped!

Being a worrier in health matters, I couldn't just forget about the lump. I became anxious. It could, after all, be cancer. No, it couldn't be. I had been married two years, had a three-month-old son, had just graduated from law school, and was about to begin my first real job. With all these beginnings, with so much of life just starting, it couldn't be cancer.

Judy, my wife, who had a realistic outlook in these matters, felt confident that the lump was not serious, but knowing me well suggested that I visit the internist to put my mind at ease. I initially rejected the idea because I was so frightened, but after weeks of tormenting both of us, I made the appointment.

In the meantime, I discussed my fears with a medical resident at Albany Medical Center who lived in the next-door apartment. He explained that enlarged lymph nodes were not uncommon but quite often could not be explained. The name for this condition was lymphadenitis. When I pressed him, the resident admitted that it could be more serious; it could be a type of lymphoma or cancer of the lymph system. The most common lymphoma was called Hodgkin's disease. He said that if he had to choose to get a type of cancer, he would pick Hodgkin's. It responded to treatment, he explained, and many patients lived with the disease for over fifteen years.

Despite his assurances that it was unlikely that I had cancer of any type, the naming of a specific disease increased my anxiety. The discussion had somehow made the prospect of having the disease more concrete, more probable. This wasn't the resident's fault. He was a warm, compassionate man who had simply answered my questions. Six months later he was going to manifest his compassion toward me in a very real, but difficult, way. He was going to have to tell me the truth.

The day for my appointment with the internist finally arrived. I was filled with trepidation as I entered his office. Dr. Dole* was a man in his late sixties, very tall, with a strong, confident face that expressed a genuine concern. He palpated the lump under my arm. "It's not very big," he said matter-of-factly.

"About the size of a peach pit," I offered.

He carefully examined my other arm and then my neck and without further hesitation he declared, "It's nothing to worry about."

"How do you know for sure?" I asked.

"Well, we don't know for sure unless it's biopsied."

"Biopsied?"

"Removed and examined under a microscope."

"Can I have that done?" I asked.

*Not his real name.

"It's not necessary," he assured me. "A swollen lymph node is not unusual. Go home and don't worry about it."

"I'll try," I said, and put on my shirt. I had come to Dr. Dole on several occasions with my heart symptoms and so I might have added, "But you know me."

I went home and fingered the lump. Once, twice, ten, twenty times a day. It was nothing. It was something. And there was only one way to find out: biopsy. I tortured myself with the morbid possibilities for several weeks. Finally, encouraged by my wife, I called the internist.

"It's starting to drive me crazy," I told him. "I don't sleep well, I can't think straight. I have to have it out."

I was surprised when Dr. Dole did not argue. He simply said, "Call Dr. Simon's* office for an appointment. He's an excellent surgeon. I'll phone his secretary to say that you'll be calling."

I was able to see Dr. Simon within a few days. The prospect of having the matter finally resolved gave me a measure of peace. Sitting in Dr. Simon's waiting room, I witnessed a scene I'll never forget. An older couple, perhaps in their sixties, were sitting next to me. The woman looked distraught; there was a crazed look in her eyes. "I know it's gotten worse," she said angrily to her husband. "You wouldn't believe me, but I know it is worse. You'll see. If he has to operate, then what? Not even fifty-fifty," she accused him. "Not even fifty-fifty," she repeated sadly.

After her examination she walked toward him with a peculiar triumphant look on her face. "I was right," she said maliciously. "The aneurysm could break at any moment. I have to have emergency surgery tomorrow morning. And you wouldn't believe me."

How terrible to be that hateful, I thought. But I could sympathize with the woman and her feelings. I resolved then to never use my fear as a club against Judy or anyone else I loved.

Dr. Simon had a reputation as a good surgeon, but I found him to be a very cold man. He seemed unaware of my anxiety and my fears. He felt the lump and asked how long it had been there. He told me that most probably it was benign, just as Dr. Dole had said. He saw very little reason for the operation.

*Not his real name.

"The reason," I explained, "is that I've been worrying about it for several weeks. It's interfering with my work, my home life, and my sleep. I want it out."

He looked quickly at a paper on his desk. "Next Tuesday," he said. "Be at the fifth-floor operating room at eight A.M. I'll do it under local anesthesia. It shouldn't take more than an hour, probably less."

My first experience with surgery was not unpleasant. I joked with the nurses and generally made light of the situation. The application of the iodine to my newly shaved armpit stung a bit, but other than that, the operation was painless. And at least I was free of the lump. As I got up off the table, I felt much better and was quite confident that the node was benign. I called the surgeon the next day. A biopsy had established the node was benign!

Relief swept through me like a springtime wind. I was clean, wholesome, well! There was no longer a need to worry, no longer a need to be preoccupied with my body, my health, my life. I could begin to live a *peaceful* life again.

Living with Ambiguity

Weeks, months went by. Then night fell again. Another lump. In the same place, the left axillary. Christ no, I thought, when I first felt it. Do I have to go through this again?

"Look," the internist said quite convincingly, "it's not unusual that another node grew there. But whatever caused the first to grow caused the second one to grow. We can't operate on you every three months. And anyway, it's not necessary."

I was examined once again by the surgeon and he agreed. Diagnosis: chronic lymphadenitis (meaning that for some inexplicable reason, my lymph nodes were swelling up).

Okay, I thought, I have to live with ambiguity.

I lived in that twilight zone for about six months. I must confess I was not very brave. It was like living with a yoke attached to my back. Sometimes I could ignore it, but I usually felt its weight. My shoulders literally slumped. I was more quiet, more introspective

than usual. I tried to appear happy with Judy and my son and sometimes was successful. But the pervading emotion during this period
was fear. Then I was back in the doctor's office.

"The lump is growing," I told Dr. Dole. "It's about the size
of a small plum. And besides, in two months I am going abroad.
I'll be living in Spain for a year. Let's take the damn thing out
again."

He felt the lump carefully and repeated what he had said six
months before. While the lump was a bit larger, it was still not significant in view of the results of the first biopsy.

"How big does it have to get before it gets significant?" I asked.

"It probably won't get much larger," he insisted. "We know that
it's not malignant. Go see Dr. Simon again and see what he has to
say, but I'm sure he'll agree that another operation is not necessary."

Of course, Dr. Simon agreed. He had operated once and the node
was negative. He had made his pronouncement: I was not ill. My
body was not going to prove him wrong.

"What if it gets bigger when I'm in Europe?" I asked.

"I don't care how big it gets," he replied. "You don't have a malig-
nancy and that's all there is to it. If you went to a physician over
there, he might be alarmed. But that's because he would not have
seen the pathologist's report of the first biopsy. My advice is to forget
about the whole matter."

I could not argue with the soundness of the advice. Putting it into
practice was another matter.

I completed a one-year clerkship at the appellate division of the
Supreme Court in June. I spent July as a volunteer attorney with an
Albany civil rights group called The Brothers. Judy and I planned to
spend a year in Spain with our fifteen-month-old son, Chris. We
could afford to do this because my father had given me $6,000 for
my education when I was in college. The stockbroker who handled
the funds had done extraordinarily well.

In less than four years our stock account had magically grown to
nearly $60,000. Then in my second year of law school a friend sug-
gested I buy a particular oil stock. I invested $10,000 and within a
year the stock split several times and then recovered its original value.
When I graduated, I was worth over $100,000. Since I had received

a full tuition scholarship to attend law school and Judy had supported us, we had never spent any of our stock money.

We had chosen Spain for several reasons: It was inexpensive; Judy spoke the language; and I loved Hemingway. I was going to write fiction, something I had begun doing in college.

We left for Europe in late August. The new life in Spain initially diverted my attention from what was under my left arm, but as the months passed I could ignore it no longer. The node was there and it was growing. I remember playing Ping-Pong one afternoon and noticing that the lump was hitting against the side of my arm when I tried to slam the ball. A few days later, I went to a British doctor in Madrid. After hearing my entire history, he said that while the lump was suspicious and would ordinarily be removed as a routine precaution, because of the previous biopsy I should wait and see.

Wait and see. Whenever I was in the presence of a doctor who was appraising my situation, I weighed not only every word he uttered, but every nuance of feeling that emanated from his tone, his manners, his gestures. Was he really more concerned than he indicated by his words? If he said "wait and see," didn't that mean that there *was* cause for concern? What was he really thinking?

The truth. Only another biopsy could determine that. Meanwhile, the lump had grown much bigger than the first node. It was perhaps the size of a lemon. And I knew. Deep down I knew. It was not like the first time. There was no underlying feeling of optimism. What was going to happen to me? *Was I going to die?* Nearly a year and a half had elapsed since the appearance of the first lump. If it was cancer, I kept thinking, then I was losing precious time in which I could have been treated. I knew the importance of early detection, and a year and a half had gone by!

But, once again, another doctor had told me not to worry. What was I supposed to do? Take it out myself? Another month passed before I went to still another doctor, a Spaniard who had been trained in England. Once again I told him the history and what all the other doctors had said. He felt the lump and looked at me directly. "I don't care what they said. It should be taken out immediately. It can be done here or you can fly home. I'm sorry to have to say this, but I think it's serious."

This was the first of many blows. I was stunned to the point of numbness. As the numbness wore off, I became deeply depressed. I vacillated between keeping a stiff upper lip and falling into an abyss of terror. Judy and I made the necessary arrangements to go home. We packed our things, arranged to ship the car we had purchased, and exchanged our ship reservations for airplane tickets. We had come over on the ship because I was quite uncomfortable about flying. Now I thought that the forced decision to fly was one of fate's tricks, a way to trap me so that the final mutilation might take place. Let it be, I thought. What difference does it make? A quick death for me or a slow one.

We arrived in New York on a cold February morning, the sixth to be exact, a Friday. We moved in with Judy's parents and told them about our worries. They were of course greatly concerned. I saw Dr. Dole on Friday afternoon. He agreed that I should have emergency surgery to have the lump removed. He called the surgeon and the operation was scheduled for Monday morning. This time there was no hesitation, no argument.

On Saturday I went to church. I was a Roman Catholic then and went to confession for the first time in a year. I told the priest about my forthcoming operation and my tremendous fear. I was almost in tears as I spoke. The priest, an older man, was more concerned with why I had not received the sacraments than with my health. He offered me no solace. I asked him to pray for me, but I knew his prayers would be useless. I spent Sunday trying desperately to distract myself from thinking about the inevitable.

I entered the hospital on Sunday night. I was depressed, worried, almost out of touch. A thick gloom seemed to encircle my body as well as my mind. I was passive, powerless. A nurse gave me a sedative. I fell asleep.

I was awakened early the next morning and given a shot to relax me. I don't remember much after that. I vaguely remember that someone was trying to put something in my throat and that at one point I tried to bite a hand that seemed to be choking me. I remember being told to count and then losing consciousness. I awoke in a room, surrounded by nurses, felt a terrible pain under my left arm, tried to express my pain, and then fell back into a deep sleep. I awoke again that evening. Judy was in the room. I don't remember what we said or how we looked at each other. I don't want to remember.

The Longest Day: Waiting for the Results

The next day was the longest day of my life. I knew that the results of the biopsy would be bad, but I wasn't sure when I would be given the information. I had been told by the nurses that it was important that I walk as much as I could—there would be less likelihood of infection or pneumonia. And so I began to pace at an early hour, before 7 A.M. I did not stop walking the entire day. I walked first in my room and then in the hall. I was expecting the worst, but I did not give up hope entirely; I prayed continually that the node would be benign. The waiting seemed endless. And since Judy was occupied with our son, I waited alone.

I looked for Dr. Dole or Dr. Simon. Both had visited me early that morning and had said they would be in to see me later in the day. But they didn't come. I kept on walking. I think I must have decided that I would not sit down until I knew.

I remember walking past the nurses' station where the patients' charts were kept. It was perhaps four o'clock in the afternoon. I knew that my chart was there and that, affixed to the chart, was the pathologist's report. But only my doctor could give me the results. The nurses had told me the rule. Now they eyed me suspiciously as I walked past them.

An hour later I saw the resident who had lived next door. He was coming from the direction of the nurses' station. I could see in his face that he had read my chart.

"Jesus Christ, Mike," I pleaded as he approached me. "I have to know. I can't stand this any longer."

"You know I can't give you the results," he said softly. "Please . . ." he started to beg.

"It's *my* goddamn body," I snapped. "Mike, the doctors may not come for hours. All day I've been waiting. Please."

"All right," he faltered. "It's Hodgkin's," he said at last. "Remem-

ber what I told you before," he added quickly. "It's a disease that can
be treated."

"Thanks," I said in a barely audible voice. "It's better that I know.
I couldn't stand not knowing."

"Some people don't take the news well," he said, looking at me
carefully. "Some people, when they hear, try to do crazy things—
jump out a window. That's why."

"I'm okay," I assured him. "I'm not going to kill myself."

I was alone again. Tears burned my eyes and I kept on asking
myself how this could have happened to me. Asking and receiving no
answer.

Judy arrived and, in a word, I told her the news. We cried together
and waited for one of the doctors to appear. Finally, around six-
thirty, Dr. Simon arrived. I searched his face for signs of grief, of sadness or compassion. His face contained no messages; he seemed tired,
in a hurry. He took us into a private room and told us the news. His
statement was flat and to the point: "The results show that you have
a form of cancer called Hodgkin's disease."

When I was able to speak, I asked: "Does it mean . . . does it mean
I am going to die?"

I will never forget his answer. Not the words so much as the way
he said them. The words almost hissed out of his mouth. He seemed
annoyed at my questions, angry with me.

"It doesn't necessarily mean you're going to die, *as you put it*. Radiation is very effective in treating the disease."

As I put it! Was there another way of putting it? Another way of
asking? Did I violate some unwritten rule by asking if I was going to
die? The man may have been a good surgeon, but he was the most
insensitive human being I had ever met.

A Pitfall: Being "Good" by Not Sharing Pain

When I recall that terrible day in the hospital, I remember the pain
of being alone. Judy was with our son Chris, who was not yet two.

Judy's parents lived in the area (we were staying with them), but both worked. My parents also lived nearby, but I had chosen not to tell them. My brother, nine years my senior, and his wife knew I was going into the hospital for a biopsy, that it could be serious, but they were about to leave on a vacation. My brother and I were very close. When I was a child, he had been a second father. His attitude was, "I know that whatever happens, you'll be all right." I also have two older sisters. One lived in Denver and the other in New York City.

I had friends I might have called upon, but the truth is I was deeply ashamed that I might have cancer. If I did, the last thing I wanted was for anyone to know. I didn't want pity. I also feared that if people knew, they would avoid me. I'd be ostracized. I told Judy, "We must keep this a secret."

This is the simple explanation of why I was alone that day until Judy's mother returned from work to take care of Chris. The explanation, however, raises more questions. Why didn't I tell my parents? My mother was sixty-six, my father was seventy-one; both were in good health. Why didn't Judy ask her mother to stay home from work for one day? Why hadn't I asked my brother or my sisters to be there? Both Judy and I would have been so much better off if we had had some support that day and in the months that followed. But we didn't know what our needs were or how to ask. It never occurred to us. To this day we feel badly about the way we compounded our own tragedy. And there is an explanation for that, too.

As children we had been taught to be compliant and obedient—good children. Not to burden other people, especially our parents. I was being a "good boy," a good son, a good brother by not making any demands, or even requests. When I look back at that twenty-seven-year-old young man from this point in my life, twenty years later, I feel sad for him. I feel sad for Judy. I think the pain would have been much easier to bear if those who loved us had been there to share it, to cushion it, to help us hold it.

I spent the next two days in the hospital recovering from the operation. I was drained, emotionally flat. My parents knew I was in the hospital and came to see me. I didn't want them to know the diagnosis because I felt it might have been more of a shock to them than they could bear. I told them everything was fine. Unfortunately, Dr.

Dole knew my father, and when he saw him in the hospital corridor he expressed his condolences. I never told my mother and she never found out.

When I saw Dr. Dole, he expressed genuine concern. "The first node was benign but the little one in back of it wasn't. That's the way it happens sometimes. I wish we had gotten to the second one." He shook his head and hurried on his way.

I had a good friend from college, Robert Young, who was training in medicine and cancer research at Yale. When I telephoned and told him the news, he said he would find out where I should go to be treated. When I spoke to him the next day, he told me not to worry—that Hodgkin's was a very treatable lymphoma. A doctor from Stanford University had been obtaining remarkable cure rates, using radiation from a 6-million-electron volt (6 MeV) linear accelerator. Quite a few medical centers in the East followed his treatment method with the same machine, and Yale was one of them. Robert suggested that as soon as I was able to leave the hospital I should go to New Haven. He would make the necessary arrangements. I agreed to leave everything in his hands.

Before leaving the hospital, I saw Dr. Dole once more. I told him about my conversation with my friend and that I had decided to go to Yale for treatment. He wished me luck and suggested that my doctor at Yale send him periodic progress reports.

When I left the hospital, I felt frail. The winter air was bitter cold; the world felt hostile. Judy was with me, but, despite her presence and her loving concern, I was alone. We die alone, I thought; a simple, painful truth. I didn't know if I was going to die. I knew only that I was going to New Haven, Connecticut. I thought of my work. Would I practice law again? Judy was two months pregnant. Would I see my second child? The cold numbed me. As I thought of the future, for the first time in my life I wondered what the word really meant.

CHAPTER 3

Treatment

T he task of recounting my story is not a pleasant one. The last
thing I feel like doing is reliving the six months I spent in New
Haven. It is impossible for me to return to those days in any real
sense. I can only reconstruct how I felt. The best way for me to pro-
ceed is to sketch in what occurred. I do have some notes I made in
those terrible days of 1969. Those are the only real evidence of what
I was feeling and thinking.

In early February 1969, I was admitted to Yale–New Haven Hospital. The purpose was to have tests to find out how far my disease
had progressed. How I hate those words, *my disease*. My medical-
school friend, Robert Young, had made quite a few inquiries around
the hospital and decided that Dr. James Fischer, then on the staff of
the Department of Therapeutic Radiology and now chief of that
department, would be the best doctor to act as my primary physician.

Learning About Hodgkin's Disease

Dr. Fischer was in his early thirties. He had both a Ph.D. and an M.D.
and was known as a good researcher and an excellent clinician: He was a
shrewd diagnostician who made difficult decisions about the best course
of treatment and yet maintained a warm rapport with his patients. He
was a tall man, with a serious but gentle manner. When we first met, he
talked to me about the disease and then about the tests that would be per-

formed at the hospital. He explained that Hodgkin's was a most treatable lymphoma, or cancer of the lymph system.

The lymph system consists of tiny vessels that run throughout the body and carry clear yellowish fluid containing white blood cells. Lymph nodes are glandlike structures lying in groups along the course of the lymphatic vessels; their function is to filter out germs and foreign bodies. When Hodgkin's is first detected in the early stages, the prognosis of complete cure is over 90 percent.

In the earliest stage—Stage One—the disease is found in only one site of the body. Thus, if tests showed there was no disease elsewhere in my body, I would be classified in Stage One. If the tests revealed disease in more than one site in the body, and if all of the disease was either above or below the diaphragm, I would be classified in Stage Two. If diseased nodes were found both above and below the diaphragm, I would be in Stage Three, and finally, if the disease was found outside the lymph system, I would be in the last and often fatal category of Stage Four.

Dr. Fischer explained that there were two other classifications: *A* and *B*. If a person did not have any "systemic" symptoms such as fever, night sweats, and general itching, he was in *A* (my position), but if he did have these symptoms, he was in *B*.

The treatment of choice for stages One-A, Two-A, and Three-A was radiation. In the last few years, statistics had shown that radiation treatment was highly successful. A Stanford radiologist, Dr. Henry Kaplan, had attacked Hodgkin's quite aggressively by applying a dosage of 4,000 rads (a rad is a unit of radiation) not only to the diseased areas, but to adjacent areas as well. He had used as the source of radiation a "6 MeV linear accelerator," the same type of machine that was presently being used at Yale. Yale was following his protocol, the course of treatment he had used, and was getting the same results: a 95 percent cure rate for Stage One-A, a 90 percent cure rate for Stage Two-A, and a 70 percent cure rate for Stage Three-A.

Dr. Fischer felt that there was every reason to believe that I was in one of the three earlier stages, and thus my prognosis was quite good. I felt relieved hearing those words. To cover other possibilities he told me that remarkable success was being obtained in treating people with Stage Four through the use of chemotherapy with a combination of drugs. The National Institutes of Health in Bethesda, Maryland, had pioneered in using the new drug combinations, and many of their patients in this last stage were free from disease as long as three to four years after treatment. In the past, the longest "remissions"—stable periods without a sign of the disease—had been only a year.

I was in the hospital for about a week. During that time I had an intensive clinical examination and a series of X rays. There were blood tests and a bone marrow biopsy. Finally there was a lymphangiogram—a procedure in which fluid is inserted into the lymph vessels in the feet and forced into the body so that the lymph nodes in the lower parts of the body, including the lower abdomen, can be X-rayed and diagnosed.

I received news of the results at a small house that Judy and I had rented outside of New Haven. Blood tests indicated that my liver was free of disease and the bone marrow was negative. Conclusion: I was not in Stage Four. The lymphangiogram was inconclusive; not much fluid had flowed into the left side of my lymph system and thus it was impossible to make a definitive diagnosis. The X rays of nodes in my lower left abdomen were considered "suspicious." When I heard that not enough fluid had gotten into the left side, I felt I knew why. The lymph vessel is extremely narrow and the doctors have to insert the fluid with an instrument as thin as a needle, a very difficult procedure. The chief of diagnostic radiology had inserted the fluid into my right foot, but a resident had worked on my left. He had spilled a great deal of the fluid even under the watchful eye of his chief.

The Importance of Knowing the Hopeful Aspects of a Prognosis

I was quite happy with the results. Even though there was a possibility I was in Stage Three, the worst the prognosis could be was a 70 percent chance of cure. The doctors at the medical center where the first biopsy had been performed had never mentioned these statistics, nor had they discussed the more hopeful aspects of prognosis. I had assumed the worst: that having cancer, it would just be a matter of time. Seventy percent was, to my mind, a very wide corridor of hope. If Dr. Simon had only discussed the possibilities of cure, how much anguish he could have prevented! I wondered if he was aware of the current research and whether he had ever heard of Henry Kaplan. A surgeon, I could not help thinking, should be more than a good technician. If it is his responsibility to inform the patient of the presence of a specific disease, he should learn how to do it: with compassion and with full knowledge of the possible treatments and the most hopeful prognosis. If he does not have the time and the compassion to perform this most sensitive function, then the responsibility should be delegated to someone else, perhaps a medical social worker.

When I saw Dr. Fischer at the hospital, he went into greater detail about the results of the examinations. Treatment was to begin in a few days. He said that since the nodes in my lower abdomen were suspicious, they would have to be biopsied. This meant a laperotomy, an exploratory into the stomach. While the surgeon was at it, he would also remove my spleen. The spleen is an organ that is part of the lymph system and is often positive for disease. Since one could live without a spleen, it was Yale's policy to remove it whenever a laperotomy was performed. I was apprehensive about undergoing another operation under general anesthesia. The operation performed just a few weeks before—a simple incision under the arm—had left me in a great deal of pain. I was also afraid of "going under," of being forced to lose consciousness; it was too much like a temporary death. I asked Dr. Fischer if the operation was absolutely necessary. He assured me that it was. He would schedule the operation for the end of April or early May, but first I was to undergo four weeks of radiation to the upper parts of my body: neck, chest, under both arms, as far down as the diaphragm. I would be given the same protocol used by Dr. Kaplan in his highly successful treatment: two hundred rads a day, a thousand a week, over four weeks on the 6 MeV. I should expect some bad side effects from the treatment. I would lose the hair on the back of my head, I would at times feel nauseated, the treatments would be tiring. Since radiation suppressed the production of new blood cells, my blood count would be closely monitored.

The next day Dr. Fischer worked with several of the radiation therapy technicians to delineate the treatment areas on my body. I was painted with the thick, red marks of a special pencil: lines on my chest, back, neck, and head. The machine was shaped like a big fat C. The large tube at the top emitted both a light beam and the radiation. The bottom part of the C was the beam stopper, which contained lead and concrete. Between the two points was a horizontal table on which I lay. The doctor placed variously shaped lead weights on the glass cylinder under the light beam of the machine until the beam focused only on those areas that were to be treated. Certain portions of the lungs had to be protected, and the head was not part of the treatment area.

The following day it was not the light beam, but beams of radiation, that the machine propelled into my body. I was told to lie perfectly still on the table, the lead blocks were inserted, the technicians left the room, and the thick, lead door closed behind them. One of the women spoke to me through a microphone. "All set. Don't move until I tell you to." Then a shrill, high-pitched noise pierced the air, indicating that the machine was operating. It was not an alarm but the sound of the flow of the powerful energy—6 million electron volts. Less than a minute later, the noise stopped and the door opened. The technicians had me turn over on my stomach and then rearranged the blocks. The door closed and once again the machine's noisy mechanism told me what it was doing.

"It's okay," I assured the machine. "Do what you have to do. Kill every one of the goddamn cells. Every single one of them."

The treatments, including the time I spent in the waiting room, took less than an hour a day. During the first few weeks, I spent a great deal of time in the Yale Medical Library reading every article I could find about Hodgkin's. I read about Kaplan's research and verified what Dr. Fischer had told me. Whenever I had any questions about what I had read, Dr. Fischer answered them. I discovered that I had contracted a strange disease. Not many years ago, it had been considered incurable, and most medical texts still said that it was. When radiologists began to treat the disease aggressively, they began to get results—long remissions, even cures. A "cure" was really a statistical definition. It meant you were free of symptoms for a period of years (either five or ten, depending on the cell type of the disease).

You had the same chance of a recurrence as someone in the general population had of getting the disease.

Statistically, women with the disease did better than men, younger people better than older. The disease was said to exist in virtually every country except one, Japan; indigenous Japanese seemed to be immune. The disease sometimes affected the immunological system, causing it to become "dysfunctional" or less able to fight off other diseases. Thus, some scientists felt that the disease was basically a disease of the immune system. There was some evidence that the disease was caused by a virus, although it was generally agreed that, like most cancers, the etiology was unknown. It was a variable disease, often unpredictable.

It was during the first few weeks of treatment that I wrote down some of my thoughts:

March 13, 1969:

Today was my ninth radiation treatment. I feel nauseated and weak. I have received 1,875 rads to my upper areas and will receive 2,000 more there. I hate the thought of it because I feel that the rays are making me sick, are killing part of me. My task in writing this journal is not defined. If it is to record all thoughts, it is impossible; if all significant thoughts, then not ambitious enough. I don't want it to be a diary but a means of exploration. I have not been given lately to introspection, except the kind that goes nowhere, is often incoherent, and leaves off in the middle of thoughts.

Driving to the hospital this morning, I sang a sort of dirge, a song that went, "I am a cancer patient, I can't help but love my body that was once pure and clean, it is after all my body."

Fear of Death? Or of Dying Unfulfilled?

Later on, I found myself struggling with an idea that has always bothered me—the fear of dying unfulfilled, not accomplishing my life's purpose, whatever that was. I finally understand, I think, the importance of, perhaps the necessity of, being happy notwithstanding the fear and notwithstanding what I term the "ax" which hangs over every person's head. That ax is the fear of death, or, more accurately, the realistic threat of death. There are also the death-axes that hang over our loved ones, which are also axes for us, but most troubling is our own personal death-ax.

To live with the overshadowing of that death-ax is not the problem, for we all must live, one way or the other. The problem is to live *well*—to live without a pervading depression, without anxiety, to live happily, confidently, productively.

I have found it difficult to live well with a normal death-ax in the past, and now I am faced with living with one that is more ominous because it is more real. I realize that should my doctor tell me that death was certain, a matter of so many months or years, I would no longer experience the threat of the death-ax. I would have to cope with actually watching it fall. To me this is a completely different kind of dread and how I would react to it I don't know. At this point, I don't have to face that question; instead I must live with the knowledge that there is a substantial chance that I shall die within the next two or three years.

I think I have been overconcerned with thoughts of death from time to time, especially in early college years. But in later years, I was not so much preoccupied with death as I was unhappy. For a long time I wanted to be not just a writer, but a successful writer, i.e., a known writer. Not achieving these goals led to free-floating feelings of unfulfillment which in turn led to low threshold feelings of unhappiness. I am now convinced that ONE CANNOT GO THROUGH LIFE *perpetually unhappy*—even the least bit—about a condition that is permanent or about which nothing can be done.

I must be happy *now*, now, notwithstanding the present lack of fulfillment in my work. I must be happy now, notwithstanding the ax over my head. This is the argument to myself. To convert the argument into an *attitude*—that is the difficult part.

March 25, 1969:
I want to write about my son Christopher, and about my obsession. I call it an obsession, but maybe the word is too strong. I must do something for my son Chris so he will remember me. I feel I have

cheated him in being sick. If I were to die, I would be robbing him of a father. In the past, the thought of Judy remarrying has disturbed me. I very selfishly want to be my son's father, to raise him. I don't want another man taking over this job, this pleasure. Yet, I fully expect that Judy would remarry, I assent to it, it would be best for her and my son. But to be just a memory for her—and less than that for him—is difficult to take. If I die, I will not have been able to express the love I have for him. I want, therefore, to somehow establish a permanent proof and expression of my love. I could set up a trust so that he would receive money when he reached twenty-one that would come directly from me. It would be better, perhaps, if Judy had control over the money, yet I have this need to give a direct gift.

I could write him a letter to be opened when he turned twenty-one. Cruel because it might be heart-rending? Meaningless, since he would never have known me? But how else to let him know how much I always wanted a son, how happy I was when he was born, how much happiness he's given me, how we played together, how before he could talk we sang together, how we shared a joke, how we would have been good friends, always, even though I was his father, how important he was, is, in my life? Would, Almighty God, that I see my son to manhood.

April 14, 1969:

It will take a long time to get down to it because right now I'm out of touch with it and don't know if I'll be able to touch it again. It's what happens in your mind when you're told you have a disease that has been demonstrably killing people since 1903, when they recognized it as a disease, and killing people without the status of a doctor's name probably thousands of years before. (I know it's "I," but using "you" diminishes me, diminishes my own involvement, although I know and don't forget that "you" is "I.") It is a variable disease, meaning that some people live longer than others, longer being fifteen years and shorter being—God, I hate to think how short "short" can be—six months, and why not three?

I have withered since they told me. Not physically, not

the CACHEXIA—that frightening word which means emacia-
tion, a wasting away and a sign the end is near. But I have withered.
Irony. I see it and it makes me wonder about things like self-
fulfilling prophecy. Eight years ago I wrote what I thought was a
novel, some 125 pages of monologue by a hospitalized young man
who discovers, and comes to grips with, the fact that he is dying of
leukemia. A literary agent thought it was good enough to handle but
thirteen publishers rejected it. Now I can't help thinking that the
Lord God bought it ("You wrote it, now live it, if you're so goddamn
smart.") More likely, being a hypochondriac, I may well have talked
myself into a disease that I can't talk myself out of.

The Operation: A Dreamworld of Pain

After the four-week treatment was completed, Judy and I returned to
Albany. For the next few weeks I rested so that I would gain the
strength needed for the operation. I did everything I could to delay
it. Whenever I spoke to Dr. Fischer by telephone, I exaggerated my
various discomforts. I managed to delay the operation for a week.
Then, in the latter part of April, I was admitted to the hospital. Judy
had said good night and had gone to stay with two close friends. I
would see her in the recovery room. About 10 P.M., the surgical resident who was to prep me for the operation examined me. "The
intern tells me you have a cough," he said.
"Yes," I assured him. "It's been with me for about three weeks,
from a cold that won't go away."
"You're also running a low-grade fever."
"From the cold," I assured him. "It's from the cold."
The resident listened to my cough, pressing the cold metal of the
stethoscope against my chest and then my back.
"I think we're going to have to delay the operation for a couple of
weeks," he said finally.
"You can delay it forever, as far as I'm concerned," I told him hap-
pily. "When can I get out of here?"

"Any time you want. I'll discharge you right now."

I leaped out of bed, shucked my pajamas, and was into my clothes in a minute. I called Judy and she met me at the hospital entrance. I felt like a bird fleeing its cage as I ran toward the car. We spent a jubilant evening with our friends in New Haven and then went to New York City instead of home to continue the celebration. It was a lovely reprieve, even if it was only for two weeks.

I feared that I would die on the operating table. I had read that 5 percent of those undergoing spleenectomies did not survive, but Dr. Fischer assured me that the 5 percent included the chronically ill and aged and that my chances were much better than the statistics indicated. Reluctantly, I reentered the hospital in early May. I was there for ten days.

I have no recollection of the day following the operation. I was under heavy sedation to combat the severe pain which during the next few days never really left me. I did not think I would live, did not really care. To combat the danger of pneumonia, I had to breathe into a bottle, a way to force me to take deep inspirations and exhalations. Every morning a technician brought the cursed device to my room and would not leave until I had taken the required number of breaths, each painful to my tender stomach where they had made the incision.

One night I was given Talwin, a painkiller, and it sent me on a hallucinogenic "trip" that lasted several hours. Whenever I closed my eyes, a thousand images would fill my mind. I seemed to be able to travel at the speed of light. I saw a tiny seedling grow into a tree and then into the head of a doctor friend who had visited me that day, and then I saw my friend before my eyes. His skin began to wrinkle, his face shriveled, until he looked in his eighties and he was no longer Caucasian but Chinese. I was in a church and the organ was alive and the music was exquisite and palpable. I could see it and smell it as well. Objects lost their form and hung or floated in Daliesque fashion.

I could stop the haunting procession of images by simply opening my eyes, and occasionally I did so. But I soon returned to that lost wonderworld where I first learned of the almost limitless possibilities of the mind.

Good News and Bad: The Completed Diagnosis

After three or four days there was a perceptible change. I felt alive again and the pain was less frequent, less taxing. I was told the results of the biopsies: The good news was that the liver had been biopsied and was disease-free; the bad news was that the disease had been found in my spleen and in nodes in my stomach and groin. The diagnosis was complete: I was a Stage Three-A. Dr. Fischer told me that I would have to undergo total-body radiation. Since I had read all the studies, I knew what he meant: two more four-week cycles of radiation, one cycle on the upper part of my stomach, the other on the lower stomach and into my groin. I had three weeks to recuperate from the operation before the first cycle would begin. Once again the results had been mixed. It could have been worse, but it could have been much, much better.

While in the hospital, I met someone from Albany. He was a psychiatric resident, call him Dr. S, and he, too, had come to Yale to be treated for Hodgkin's. He'd had his spleen removed a few days before I had, and when he was ambulatory he came to visit me to assure me that I would be feeling a little better the next day. His spleen was negative and they had found no disease in his stomach, but there were positive nodes in his groin and neck, so he was also classified in Stage Three-A.

Dr. S and I spent quite a lot of time together in June and later on in July and August. We were able to discuss our feelings and we certainly understood each other. In July 1969, I wrote the following:

July 28, 1969:
I was awaiting my turn at the machine, standing half-naked, draped in a sheet, when I saw Dr. S. He was standing, back away, looking at his chart. He turned at my hello.

"Not a very good weekend," he said coming over. "Bad news." It was his liver, he explained. It was palpable. Which meant it was able to be felt. Which meant it was swollen. Which meant it might be infiltrated by the disease.

"What a goddamn disease," he said.

"Like a goddamn ax over your neck all the time," I said. I had forgotten all about the ax. Now it was there again, looming as large as
ever, big enough to hang over both Dr. S's neck and my own. He
had to have another liver biopsy. An overnight in the hospital. Two
months ago we had both had one done and the results had been negative. He pointed four fingers. Stage Four.

"That's it. If it's that, that's it."

I walked into the room with the machine and he said, "I'll let you
know."

"Yeah, let me know," I answered.

Now I have to reassure myself. That was him. This was me. It happened to him, not me. My liver is not palpable. Only last week, it
was felt, wasn't it? Didn't Dr. Fischer feel there? He must have felt
there and it was all right. So it's okay. That was him. This is me. Jesus
Christ, what a disease, he said, I said, I say.

Please God, let me keep this hope alive. I have this hope which I
live on and it can be all right, but if it's in the liver, it's all over. Don't
let it get to my liver.

I have prayed, too, for Dr. S, but I cannot pray as hard for him as
I pray for myself. He, too, has a wife, a son. God, give us a break.
We can beat this thing, with luck. We need your help.

I think of Hemingway, stepping over bomb-holes in Madrid or in
London, waiting for a shell to dodge. We are not so brave as to go
out to danger, but inside us there is a time tomb that could blow hell
out of us. At any moment. And the moment could last for two years.
Two years to think about it all. Two years to make peace with God
or to make a pact with the devil. Two years to cry, laugh, and cry
again. Two years to feel sorry for yourself or to stop feeling sorry for
yourself. Two years to envy the healthy. Two years to cut the veins
in your wrist. Two years to tape them up.

After I completed my second cycle of radiation, we left our rented
house outside of New Haven and moved back to Albany. I called my
old boss, the chief administrative officer at the appellate division, and
told him my situation. Although I felt uncomfortable telling him
about my illness, I wanted to work. He offered his condolences and
then arranged for me to do legal research for the court. He allowed

me to do the work at the Yale Law Library for the period I had to be in New Haven.

In July, I spent the weeks in New Haven and drove home on weekends. The days were lonely. My friend Robert was away for the month. I missed Judy and Chris. Except for my stay in the hospital this was the first time we had been apart. Sometimes I slept in the medical dormitory, other times at the home of my friends, the Cains.

Each morning after receiving my radiation treatment, I would go to the law library. The radiation to the lower abdomen often nauseated me, but I was able to control the sick feeling by keeping a little food in my stomach. Working kept my mind occupied. I have to concentrate, I told myself, I'm doing this to support my family. But the fearful thoughts would still come: *Soon the treatment will be over. What will happen then? How will I be able to live? What if, what if, what if?*

CHAPTER 4

—————————————————————

Remission/
Recurrence

I n August 1969 I completed my third four-week cycle of radiation
therapy. On the thirtieth of that month, my second son was born.
I witnessed his birth; after the long waiting, first his head popping out
(looking up at the world, not down) and then after a painful thrust
his tiny shoulders and then his torso seeming to inch out and finally,
finally (what was he?) a boy! I saw his sex before the doctors and
shouted happily.

The event of my son's birth, as joyous as it was, took place beneath
a cloud. Yes, I had another son. But would I be able to fulfill my
implicit promise to him: to father him until his manhood? I believed
strongly that biological fatherhood was relatively insignificant; a man
fathered a child by his acts after the child was born. More than anything I wanted to see my children into manhood, to be truly their
father.

When I was discharged from Yale–New Haven Hospital, I was
told that I would have to return for checkups every two months. Judy
and I, with Chris, who was twenty-eight months old, and the baby,
whom we named David, settled into a new home in Albany. I began
practicing law. I continued to insist that my illness be kept a secret.
People who were curious about why we had moved to New Haven
for six months were told I was undergoing special treatment for my
psoriasis. After the first radiation treatment, I had lost the hair in the

back of my head, but by the time we moved back to Albany, it had
grown back.

Still, I remember often feeling paranoid that people knew. I have
a distinct memory of an attorney acquaintance walking toward me in
downtown Albany. When he was about fifty feet away, he noticed
me, stopped, and crossed the street. I felt like a leper.

Dreading that the Disease Would Recur

No one except Judy knew how I really felt. On the surface, things
were normal. But underneath I could characterize my life with one
word: dread. I was terrified that the disease would return. I tried to
take refuge in the statistics. I did have a 70 percent chance of cure.

Yet it was like a presence, this dread, this terrible possibility, like
a physical appendage to my body. I went to sleep with it, it invaded
my dreams; I woke with it, carried it through the day. How many
times I sat on the foot of my children's bed and cried until I shook.
There were few truly happy days or hours. For no matter how good
the moment, my joy was limited, earthbound. Oh, to have the freedom to laugh without chains, to feel, if only for a moment, a pure
happiness. But there were no such moments. I tried, but I did not
know how to live well. And so I lived a half-life.

My bimonthly checkups came much too quickly. When X rays
were taken I would have to wait a day or two for the results, and
those days were spent in terror. When Dr. Fischer called to say that
everything was fine, I was swept with a magnificent relief that lasted
for days. Then the everyday dread would return.

I knew from some of the studies I had read that if I went two years
following the beginning of treatment without any sign of disease, the
chances were about 95 percent that the disease would never return.
This was one of Kaplan's conclusions, based on his experience with
total-body radiation. In September 1970, about six months before
my two years would have elapsed, I felt a small lymph node under
my right arm. I went to see Dr. Fischer almost immediately. He felt

it carefully and said that he didn't think it was significant. It was too small. But it would have to be watched.

In October I broke out with a rash on the right side of my upper back, along the shoulder, then on my chest. The next day, when the rash began to blister, I described the condition to my internist, Dr. Dole. He told me I had something called "shingles," or herpes zoster, and that I was in for some severe pain. I asked him if shingles could cause a slightly enlarged lymph node. His answer: Definitely yes. I was ecstatic. Pour on the pain! It wasn't Hodgkin's. That was all that mattered. As Dr. Dole had promised, the pain came, grew from bad to excruciating, confined me to bed for over ten days. Eventually it passed.

But the node remained, grew larger. Dr. Fischer could not understand it. It did not feel malignant to him. In late December, however, he decided that it had to be removed and biopsied. I went to Yale in January for an operation which the surgeon did under local anesthesia. Two days later I was given the results: The node was positive. The surgeon told me he hoped it was just a minor recurrence, one that could be treated locally with radiation. But I would have to enter the hospital for further tests. What about the statistics? What were my chances? Well, the statistics (I know, I had read them, too), they weren't too good. Then again, it would depend in great part on whether the disease was found in other places in the body. And in the final analysis, people survived or they didn't. Statistics did not say anything about an individual case.

The news was crushing, brutal. What was I going to do now? In February 1971 I started to write another diary. It became too painful for me and so I stopped before the end of the month. Here are my notes from the aborted February 1971 diary.

February 1, 1971:

I never wanted so much not to write something like this. I'm not sure how far I'll get or what value it will have. Now that the disease has come back and my mind is so confused and so clear, I feel my thoughts should be written down. I know they will never come again; certainly not after I am cured, if I am cured. There would be other thoughts then, constructed thoughts; I would have to hypothesize my feelings, much like in fiction.

I don't want to write this. I would much prefer to bury myself in a novel, reading, not writing (for in writing, there are too many pauses and between these pauses, terrible thoughts creep in). And this is even worse—dealing with it head-on. I am not sure I can do it. To focus on what has happened to me makes me feel so full of anger and hate that my hands feel silly pecking away at a typewriter when what I really want to do is strangle someone. But I am a writer and a writer must write. Honesty. Honesty is an essential ingredient of good writing. So let this be honest no matter how badly it makes me look. No one writes about dying. Well this is about the worries of dying (not about dying; I can't be dying).

Right now my right armpit is burning. That's where two lymph nodes were biopsied last week. I waited days for the results.

Hearing the News Was Like Being Smashed on the Head with a Sledgehammer

Whenever the results of tests are long in coming, it is a tip-off that it's going to be bad news. This past August I had a node removed from near my right elbow. The next day the surgeon called to tell me it was negative. What a feeling that was; the load disappearing and I was able to breathe again. But this time, there was no next-day news. It was three days before Dr. Fischer telephoned: "I have very bad news for you." Very bad news. How weak the words. What the words lacked, he made up for with his tone of gravity and concern. Though I had suspected this result, still it was like being smashed on the head with a sledgehammer. I began to ask questions with a severe stutter. I could have controlled that stutter, I think. If I tightened myself up and thought of some word like "dignity" or "take it like a man." Instead, I let myself be reduced to a little child, a very scared little child.

I must go back into the hospital for more tests. It is important to determine whether the disease has spread. Two years ago the extent of my disease had been wide, but it was not outside of the lymph system. It was found not only under my left arm, but in my spleen and in nodes in my stomach. Most important it was not in my liver or bone marrow.

Now it is a new beginning and no one knows where it is. I am awaiting a call from the hospital. As soon as a bed is free, I will be admitted for a week while several tests are performed. One will be a needle biopsy of my liver. Another will be a biopsy of the bone marrow. If either is positive, then the necessity for chemotherapy. If they are negative, then the radiologists will still have the chance to perform their miracles. And there will be hope. As I write this, I am in the middle of the eye of this thing looking out. I am not concerned anymore with the past, only with the tests that may begin tomorrow. Even the old waiting is in the past now; there is only the new waiting.

February 2–5 1970:

The agony of these days, of the waiting. I was admitted to the hospital after several days of waiting until a bed was available. I arrived late in the afternoon so no tests were done that day. Only more waiting. A visit from my sister. Trying to sleep amid the snores and moans of three sick and much older men.

The next morning, more waiting. I try unsuccessfully to read. My mind keeps returning to the question, What shall I do if the disease is outside the lymph system? How shall I be able to live knowing I will probably die? You see, if there is a corridor of hope, you can live in it. Two years ago, when I had gotten the disease, there was this corridor. It was 70 percent wide and I could live in it. There were even times of happiness. After all, it was a 70 percent chance that the disease would never come back. I would picture a pie and how much 70 percent of it was. A big hunk. So much bigger than 30 percent. I had a big corridor of hope. I need a corridor of hope in order to live.

It is afternoon. I've been taken to the radiation department clinic for the bone marrow biopsy. I had this same procedure done two years ago and I remember it as absolutely painless. My memory, it turns out, is very bad. It is quite painful when the resident sticks the needle into my hipbone and withdraws the marrow, does it again. It feels like, well, she is sucking out the very marrow of my bones.

Before they can perform the liver biopsy, they have to determine the rate at which I stop bleeding. When the technician comes to test me, I offer her my finger. She rejects it. My arm?

"No," she says, "Your ear."

It seems barbaric but she proceeds to hold my tender earlobe and then—rip—cut it with a razor. She waits for the blood but there is none. Since this minor assault on my body is painful, I am not eager for her to repeat it. But she does, the same place and a new hurt. This time it bleeds and she times me with a stopwatch until I stop bleeding.

"Was my time good?" I ask.

"Yes," she assures me. I had stopped in about two minutes. Since eight is the outside limit (all the blood in your head drains out your earlobe and you bleed to death), I will be allowed to take the liver biopsy.

Again the Terrible Waiting

I am now in a private room. The wait begins anew. The results of the bone marrow test will take twenty-four hours. A doctor—the one who will perform the liver biopsy—visits me. After a thorough physical examination he goes into great detail regarding my history. He has read my chart and is familiar with the details of past illnesses. Upon examining my liver, he remarks that it is not enlarged and that this is a good sign. Not enlarged. I knew he'd been testing for that. His words helped to carry me through the day.

Yet, it is a day seemingly without end. I cannot seem to ward off new throes of anxiety and dread. I resort to prayer. I cry, I try to reconstruct my shattered world. No, the liver is not enlarged. That is a good sign. It will not be positive. I will be all right. I refuse all sleeping pills because I want to remain alive, i.e., conscious, as long as I can. Nevertheless, I sleep. It is 9 A.M. The liver doctor has just administered the novocaine into the shell of the liver and then biopsied, with a needle, a sample as big as a pin. It was painless because the liver is so big and the sample so small. How accurate is the test? About 80 percent, he answers. The results? Before the end of the day. Again, the waiting. Judy arrives and we help each other to wait. Talking, reading, dozing. I call Dr. Fischer in the early afternoon but he has left the hospital for the day. That means I will not learn the results of the liver test until tomorrow. I am relieved.

Meanwhile I wait for the resident to appear with the news of the bone marrow test. But she doesn't come. If the liver results are negative, the liver doctor, a sensitive person probably aware of my agony, might bring me the results. If he doesn't show up, does that mean the results are positive?

At four o'clock, I spot him standing at the door, very unassuming, as if he had come by mistake; perhaps it is his Oriental way (he is Thai), but he acts as if he is intruding. He asks how I am and then in a soft voice says that my liver is okay. I have to ask him: It was negative? Because from the way he says it, the meaning does not come through. Yes, it is negative. Tears flood my eyes; I shake his hand and hug Judy, who had the same problem in grasping the meaning of what he had said.

Negative. It is something to savor. I begin to praise my liver, saying that I knew it would not throw me in. No, my liver and I have a type of rapport. My liver is okay. After all, liver contains the word *live*.

The good news cushions me throughout the evening. If it is not in the liver, then it would be unlikely to be in the bone marrow (the liver doctor had said that). I repeat it over and over, like a good-luck charm.

Every time I begin to drift into sleep, I am awakened by the nurse taking my blood pressure. Finally, without much sleep having intervened, morning comes. Morning is when it is light and safe to sleep. I fall into it rather deeply.

Judy arrives about the time I awake. We pace the hall, sit in the visitor's waiting area. It is getting so I can't stand it. I know they will be coming at any time to take me for a lymphangiogram, a procedure which I had had two years before. It will take several hours and Dr. Fischer might leave the hospital before I get back and I might not learn the results of the bone marrow biopsy for another day. Besides, my time formula for bad results is starting to bother me. The longer the time after the tests, the greater the chance for bad news. With the liver, good news had come right away.

When they come to take me away about 1 P.M., I refuse to go until I telephone Dr. Fischer. His secretary reports that he is out to lunch. I envision a different scene: he, telling her in a whisper what to say as he holds the positive bone marrow results in his hand. After all, he wouldn't want me to go through the lymphangiogram, during which I have to lie still for two hours, after getting bad news. So this is it. I'm finished. They wheel me away and I think of jumping up and walking out of the hospital; after all, what's the use? But then optimism, as if working its way through sludge, begins through my efforts to surface. The liver man had said the disease probably wouldn't be there. Yet I feel no affinity with my bone marrow, as I do with my liver. It is too damn diffuse to have affinity with. Scattered here and there, how can you speak to it? How can you control it?

They poke needles containing dye between my toes and that hurts a little, enough to take my mind off my bone marrow. The dye enters some lymph vessels, the lymphangiogram doctor (the technician had told me he had done nothing but for two years in England; better that he practiced on them, I think) begins to probe (after anesthesia, it is painless) for a vessel through which the dye can be sent into the lymph system. He does this with great skill and before long both feet are hooked to the machine injecting the dye.

The radiology resident comes into the room. Her coming, obviously, has something to do with me (I am the only patient here). She must know the results of the bone marrow test. Usually she responds to me in a friendly fashion; now, she does not look at me. I do not want to ask. Finally I can bear the agony of the almost-knowledge no longer and I call across the room: "Any more results?"

"Yes," she answers, "your liver function tests are negative."

I wait out the long pause, inwardly cursing. Do I have to ask? Apparently I do. "What about the bone marrow?"

The words seem to catch in her teeth as she turns directly to me. "Those tests aren't back yet."

Lying bitch! I shout inside. All of my paranoic antennae have already given me the answer. "Look," I want to tell her. "Just tell me;

that's all. Make it easier on me and tell me." But she has left the room.

At last there is enough fluid in me. The doctor carefully takes out the needles and stitches up my feet. Then I am told to walk around to work the fluid up higher and I will be given X rays. I walk at a madman's pace up and down the hall. After several times up and down the corridor, I am told by a nurse that it is enough, but I continue to pace, to prove, if nothing else, that I can still walk fast (that should count for something, shouldn't it, you, with all your tests).

Finally, I am X-rayed and then wheeled back to my room. This is an interesting hospital phenomenon. The patient's chart always goes with the patient. But it is forbidden for the patient to read his chart. When the attendant pushes the chair there is no place to put the chart, so it is handed to the patient. If the patient begins to read his chart, the attendant says, "Hey, man, the rules say you can't do that."

When he says this to me, I reply, "Screw the rules. It's my body, so who should know more than me, right?"

"Right," he answers.

So I flip through the chart just to violate the rule. I already know what's in there.

When I arrive on the floor, I am ready to do battle with someone (the fear is fermenting into anger). Then I see Judy running down the corridor, yelling something. As she gets closer, I hear, "It's all right! It's all right!"

"What's all right?" I have to ask.

"Your bone marrow," she says. And joyously we bound down the hall to my room wanting to shout to the world: "It's all right!" Inside, I collapse into her arms and sob as deeply as I have ever sobbed. Oh, how much I want it all to come out so that my mutilated psyche can be whole again.

Then it is hustle and bustle, Judy running down to the desk to sign me out, me getting dressed. I am so weak I cannot even do that without resting. Judy had gotten the good news from Dr. Fischer, whom she had seen in the corridor. He had left her with the comforting conclusion that things looked good; that even if it were in the groin, it was still very local and could be treated with radiation. This is all that I can hope for.

An aide comes to take me away in a wheelchair. At first I think of balking, but Judy insists I sit in the chair and be wheeled to the door; another hospital rule. I want to protest that I am carrying a suitcase and attaché case, rather awkward while sitting in a wheelchair. Moreover, it is sleeting out and I have to walk in *that* with both arms full, so why can't I walk down a very dry hospital corridor? Bundled up, balancing the cases, I sit and the attendant wheels. A small crowd is in the entranceway of the hospital waiting for a ride or simply for the weather to clear and they, of course, notice the invalid holding two cases. Without uttering so much as a Captain Marvel I get up from the wheelchair and walk out into the rain and sleet.

February 11, 1971:

So much to write, so much to be said. I am back home in Albany. The tests are all in. It could have been worse; it could have been better. As far as the tests could determine, it was not in my liver or bone marrow and not out of the lymph system. But some positive nodes were found in my lower abdomen. Yesterday I was to have had a groin node removed, but that was cancelled; it is assumed that the groin area has diseased nodes, since it is so close to the area where nodes were found to be positive. Dr. Fischer is not quite sure what treatment I should have. I cannot be radiated like I was two years ago. One reason is that there is a chance of bad side effects in those areas previously treated; in the intestines, it might cause ulcers. These, he said, could be surgically corrected: cut out the ulcerated part and sew you back together. More dangerous is the effect on the spinal cord: It could be effectively severed, which would mean loss of function below that point. Other complications are possible, including death. But the likelihood of all of these are less than 25 percent, he estimated. So that if it were just a question of risk, he would tell me the risks and then try to convince me to take them.

But there is more. Because of the extent of the recurrence, because it is not confined to one or even two areas, my doctor suspects that it is elsewhere. If he's correct, then localized radiation would not work in the long run. He suggests, then, chemotherapy.

When I heard the word on the telephone, I felt like it was a death sentence. I was being discarded into that last pail reserved for Stage Fours, where all there is is hope, not data showing successes, only hope.

With chemotherapy, they are getting three-year remissions. The primary study is at the National Institutes of Health, where a four-drug combination is administered. There is hope that they might produce cures with this new combination, but hope is not the same as a statistically proven result.

I told Dr. Fischer that I did not want to be treated with chemotherapy. After all, I was not a Stage Four. But he pointed out that I was not a Stage Three, either—at least I could not be treated as one. He told me that at Yale they were treating Stage Fours with both radiation and chemotherapy, giving only a half dose of the radiation in the hopes that this would kill off most of the disease, and that chemotherapy would kill off the rest. This is what he suggests be done with me.

I have read enough of the articles to know that half a dose—2,000 rads—is simply not enough; but the theory of combining treatments is feasible. And so that's what I'll do. The idea of being bedridden for the rest of my life, however short it may be, is not acceptable. It may be better to hedge, as the doctor puts it. But I must find out the chance of spinal cord damage with 2,000 rads. Since I don't think I will beat this anyway, I would prefer to live on my feet.

The Problem of Living with the Knowledge We Are Dying Is Universal

My dreams have a way of stating things not in verbal or even pictorial form, but in a very high abstraction which makes itself felt. The night before last I came away from my dreams with the feeling (no story, no nothing) that I was in trouble and that my situation was ambiguous; and so it is. Last night it was clear to me from my dreams that things would never be the same again. I was aware of a very sharp dividing line separating two distinct things. The dividing line, I interpret, is between two different states of knowledge. There is the knowledge that I have a disease, which, having gone this far, has often been fatal. There is also the knowledge that I am at this moment alive. It is almost like being alive and dead at the same time, and the contradiction seems so big to be ludicrous. So, I may be dying; yet I am living. My dilemma, obviously, is not unique; not to me or to the class of people with fatal diseases. For certainly we are all dying; but yet we are all living. The immediacy of my situation defines, illuminates the problem. But the problem is universal.

For people whose death is at least decades away, perhaps there is no problem. Or it is a problem that need not be thought about, and maybe that is the best way of dealing with it. But there are others, too many others, with the immediate problem; the rest must face it someday.

February 12, 1971:

My friend Robert, who now has a Ph.D. in pharmacology as well as an M.D., and who is taking a residency in oncology, called yesterday after speaking with several chemotherapists. He feels that it should be chemotherapy alone. He has heard of four-year remissions using just chemotherapy and these cases are possibly cures, but the sample is small. Because radiation has gotten proven cures, I'm in favor of it, but severing the spine . . .

Right now I want to cry but I'm depleted even of tears. I've cried over these same things before, what I call the unutterable horror of it all. It is uttered but it remains in a place where words cannot reach. There are no words for my love for Judy and the boys. There are no words for my wanting to remain with them. There are no words for the horror when I think of Judy, raising the boys without me. There are no words in hell.

And yet—if there were only an "and yet," something that I could say of think that would arc up from this, bringing me to a brighter world. But there is nothing.

Last night there were no dreams I could remember. I woke up several times during the night and wanted to quickly return to notknowing. The knowledge hits you smack upon the slightest awakening and it is "unacceptable." You cannot live with that. So you try desperately to bury yourself in sleep. And it works until the next awakening. When it is morning, a new cycle begins. When it is clear that there can be no more sleep, so that that direction of escape is cut off, you realize that it cannot be. I think unspoken thoughts: I cannot go on living with this. I cannot. I think about shooting myself in the head, not so much to test the idea but to convey, I think, the idea of the only alternative. It seems absurd to say that you cannot go on living unless you are prepared to kill yourself. What I mean to say is that there are only two choices: to live or to die. And living means, at the least, getting dressed, washing up, brushing your teeth, eating breakfast, and, beyond that, doing that which you should be doing—in my case, writing, giving my sons love and attention, playing their games and teaching them, loving Judy, and, if the need arises, being attentive to others.

The First Glimmering That I Could Help Fight My Disease

February 15, 1971:

I almost gave up the idea of writing this. It came to me that my outlook was very wrong. It was as if I was accepting the fate of death. I realize that I must never do that. I must believe that I am going to kill the disease in me. For I have read enough to understand that the chemicals alone, the radiation alone, will not do it. The body itself must kill that which science cannot. The problem: how to so engage the body. How can you command your cells into battle? To be sure, I don't know, have very little idea. But first, my mind must lead, insisting to these cells that the battle can and will be won. Then I am going to pray daily that I will kill it and I will try to rely on my prayers for some peace of mind. While I am not convinced that any of these methods will work, I know I would be a fool not to try them. I realize that this attitude is improper; that it is most important to *believe* that what you're doing will work. My state of mind in all these areas falls short of belief. I see them as avenues that may or may not lead somewhere.

February 18, 1971:

Dr. Fischer called. He consulted with other experts on Hodgkin's disease. The general consensus is that I should be treated only with radiation. He said that he would do whatever I wanted, but it was still his recommendation that I first be given the chemotherapy and later a reduced dosage of radiation. He said if he were to only radiate, he would take the dosage to 3,000 rads; if I had the chemotherapy, he would try 2,500 rads. I am in favor of getting the "most" treatment and so I am going along with his recommendation.

There is also the decision of where the chemotherapy should be done. I am told there is an excellent chemotherapist locally. The alternative seems to be to go to NIH in Maryland. There, with the MOPP protocol (MOPP standing for four different drugs), the best results have been obtained. The protocol could be duplicated here. Of course, it would be much more convenient, not to mention much less expensive, to have it done here, but these cannot be considerations. The question is whether there are any medical advantages to having it done at NIH. From what I am able to understand, the only ones might be that the NIH people, being more familiar with the protocol, might be able to administer it more vigorously, especially if complications arise. Also, NIH is better equipped to deal with emergencies, as it has sensitive monitoring equipment and special rooms. For example, if the white blood count falls to a dangerously low level so that I would be susceptible to infection, they could put me in a sterile room to lessen the chance of infection. Dr. Fischer says that the chance of my needing their special equipment is small, especially if I have a good chemotherapist, as it is his job to make sure that the blood count does not fall that low.

Both Judy and I spoke with Dr. Fischer on the telephone for over forty-five minutes. I could not imagine a better doctor. He tells us as much as it will benefit us to know and he most thoughtfully tells us what he would do if it were him. I see him more as a person than as a doctor and this is a good thing. And conversely, I feel like a person, not a patient.

A Cancer Patient Can Easily Feel Isolated, Dependent, and Helpless

A patient, particularly a cancer patient, can very easily become isolated from other people. In a hospital, it almost necessarily happens. You become helpless, dependent upon others to help you perform life's basic functions. And beyond that, you have concerns that no other person has. You are concerned about your very life. Thus you cannot understand—that is, it seems so strange and alien—that the world continues at its regular frivolous pace. The television shows that are so silly to begin with become obscenely so. And you cannot help envying the obviously carefree people. Theirs is a different world, as clearly different as if they lived in the sunlight and you in the dark.

At home it is somewhat easier to blend back into the regular world for brief periods. When I play with my boys, I forget. Or I can become absorbed in a good movie. But reading is somewhat difficult. While truly it is not, I feel it is a waste of precious time, time that is being consumed much too fast as it is. I feel it is much more important that I do what I am doing now, putting my thoughts in order, transcribing them. Painting the upstairs, a task I have been meaning to do for a year, is now a priority. It seems important that I place my mark on things. I believe the idea of doing something physical has other meaning for me. It indicates, I suppose, that my body is still working; that I can't be that bad. I realize it is not very rational, but I am willing, if the endeavor is constructive, to try to comfort that part of me that words do not reach—the id, the little boy, the emotional, call it what you will. For this same reason I am beginning to exercise to attempt to get into good physical shape; not that this will cure me or even help, but it will make me feel, psychologically, better (how I can be dying with a strong body?).

February 20, 1971:

I was surprised when Dr. Fischer called yesterday to tell me that he had decided on giving me radiation first. I had read that chemotherapy following radiation must necessarily be cut down. The study I had read indicated at least six months had to elapse after radiation before successful chemotherapy could begin. Another study indicated that eighteen months was the important lapse period, that those patients who received chemotherapy within a year simply could not tolerate the protocol. Later in the day I called Robert to ask his opinion. He was emphatic that chemotherapy should precede radiation at least until 75 percent had been completed. His rationale was this (and this reflected the view of chemotherapists): First, radiation in my case had failed once. Since I would be getting even a smaller dose than before and over a much smaller area, it was most likely that it would fail again. Second, since the disease that had been found was quite spread out, from my right armpit to my left groin, it seemed probable that there was further disease somewhere that the radiation was not going to hit. Therefore, I had to rely on chemotherapy as the primary treatment. If I had any reserve left after that, then I could have radiation.

Of course, the argument made good sense. I was/am afraid that without close to full toxicity in chemotherapy I might not be able to get even a good remission. With a full drug treatment, I might even be cured. And it seems clear that following radiation I am not going to be able to get a full protocol of chemotherapy.

During the night (it was a long night), I was very absorbed in "thinking" without my being aware of words; and I came away with a "conclusion." I had fashioned a formula: that what I want is to maximize the chance of receiving the maximum amount of both treatments. I telephoned Dr. Fischer and told him how I felt. Since the chemotherapist thought radiation would definitely inhibit his treatment, shouldn't chemotherapy come first?

He disagreed. First, he said that if a chemotherapist were to tell him that there definitely would be a great amount of inhibition, he would be lying; it was simply unknown. It was known that there would be some interference, but how much, no one could say. Second, he felt, admitting his bias, that it was important to go after the known disease with the most effective agent. It was only speculation that the disease was elsewhere and the chemotherapy should be reserved for speculation. He said he would feel terrible if after three years I got the disease back because he had not given enough radiation, which was known to cure; chemotherapy was not. The fact that 4,000 rads was not enough before might very well be a statistical phenomenon; that is, it was known that in every treated area, the disease has a 5 percent chance of returning. I might have hit that 5 percent in one or more areas, which in turn began to seed other areas. With 2,500 rads, the same five percent chance of recurrence might apply. When he got finished, while I could not entirely escape the approach-avoidance conflict between the two sequences, I felt it best to defer to his judgment. After all, I was going after a cure, not a remission.

I also expressed my concern that the disease was spreading while we waited for decisions to be made. He said this was always a possibility but that the disease had been there for two years and a few more days wouldn't matter.

I mentioned to Dr. Fischer that I was taking notes on the experience. He remarked that my interest in my disease was rare among patients; that most, even educated and/or intelligent ones, want to know little or nothing. He felt it was a good thing for a person to learn about his disease and said that he always was open to questions on any level. But most did not ask.

I can understand that attitude. Yet, I am afraid not to know. Afraid that the doctors will perhaps miss something. Something staring them in the face. Thus I ask silly questions and make silly proposals; for example, Why can't you just remove all my lymph nodes in a series of operations? There's a finite number so that you should be able to get them all. And even if you get only half, you've taken away half the disease at least, maybe all of it. My doctor replied that the surgeons simply would miss too many and the procedure would be worthless. I can't help thinking to myself, What's wrong with the surgeons? Let them use a magnifying glass, take their time, and dig them out. And there are other reasons for my interest, I am sure. One I am aware of is that having knowledge gives the impression, at least, of control. If I knew everything there was to know about the disease, maybe I could control it.

February 24, 1971:

Radiation has begun. I voiced my most immediate fear to Dr. Fischer: damage to the spine. He said he thought that only the lower part of the spine might be in the treatment area—the first lumbar vertebra and below, which is not true spinal cord and would be less likely to be affected by radiation.

Today the map of treatment was clearly drawn; this process took over an hour. From what I can see, the treatment area drawn on my back extends at least two inches above the first lumbar, which means my true spine is being radiated and I am deeply worried. Yesterday I asked Dr. Fischer about avoiding it. He said he could go in from the sides, but this would necessitate hitting a lot of gut area that is not hit when one radiates from anterior to posterior and vice versa. I will ask him if it would be wise to at least split the dosage, i.e., put 1,200 rads in through the sides. The thought of being bedridden and sexless is too depressing to think much about.

Driving the 120 miles each way yesterday left me overly tired and last night was another one of those nights when I did not remember sleeping. So often in the night I am aware of being awake. At one point I felt the moistness of my chest and armpits. I was aware that my sleep was conditional upon something, but I did not know what. I could not sleep, it seemed, until something happened and it never did and perhaps (a vague recognition) it never will.

I had to be here this morning at 10:30 A.M. and so left the house at 7:30. The roads were better than yesterday and I was making good time when something very strange happened. I found myself (more than the automobile) out of control and the car was veering off the road. I was able to correct, but unable to figure out whether it was me or the car that had momentarily stopped functioning. I had been thinking about something so I don't think I had dozed; rather, it seemed like a momentary loss of consciousness.

Because it was the first day, the treatment took nearly an hour. Blocks had to be found to fit the exact pattern Dr. Fischer had outlined on my body. The technicians (women from eighteen to twenty-five) are the ones who actually do the treating; it is a most exacting job. They had a great deal of trouble setting me up because the doctor wants to keep the beam more confined than usual. The upper right axillary presented no problem; preparing the lower area from my groin to an area approximately two inches above my navel was difficult. There, now outlined in heavy red ink, is an inverted Y, with the V of the Y going down each leg past the testicles. The same outline was made on my posterior side.

After radiation I ate lunch; but then I felt on the verge of collapse and a bit nauseated. I went to sleep for a couple of hours in the medical dorm (where I am spending the night in a "borrowed" room) and then took an hour's walk through New Haven. The nausea eventually cleared up and I was able to eat a good supper. Now I am alone with danger and fear, with fatigue, with worry, with hurt. Judy is alone with our sons, and she is lonely and worried. My oldest son Chris asks where his daddy is. When I go here, I always tell him I am going to work. I don't want him to know even the word that denotes the awful truth. It is an awful business, and I can't help feeling bitter that it should be me, that it should be anyone. I am in danger and I will live with it because I have no choice. If only salvation could be gained in some simple way, like murdering a thousand devils. Then at least I could fashion a weapon and set out.

CHAPTER 5

The Revelation

The radiation treatments continued for about three weeks. I received about 2,500 rads, the maximum dosage Dr. Fischer was willing to risk. I was to rest a month and then begin chemotherapy with an Albany oncologist. I was not worried about the chemotherapy at that time, but about the possible effect of the radiation on my spinal cord. It was difficult not to think about the 5 percent chance that one day I would wake up paralyzed. Could it happen while I was walking down the street? What were they symptoms?

On the last day of the radiation treatment, I took my family to Florida for two weeks in the sun. We were there about a week when one day while I was walking down the sidewalk I bent over to pick something up and felt pins and needles shooting down my spine and into my legs. Was this the beginning? I tried bending again. I felt the same sensation, but it was not as pronounced. I tried walking some more and then bent over and felt the pins and needles once again. For several days I walked, bent over, experienced the strange sensation. Wasn't this the same sensation I had after the first treatment with radiation? I thought so, but I couldn't be sure. I telephoned Dr. Fischer and he told me not to worry: It was a common symptom following radiation and it was not associated with spinal injury. I asked, How long would it be before I *knew* there would be no damage? Again he reminded me of the unlikelihood of spinal cord damage. If it did occur, it might not show up for a year.

A year to worry, I thought. No, that was crazy. I could not worry for a year. By this time in my life, I was growing tired of worrying.

Preparing for the Message

I spent a great deal of time on the beach thinking. My body tanned. I watched my children play in the sand. I began to jog, although I could not go more than a hundred feet the first few days. I believe it was during this period that my mind was preparing for the message I was to receive when I returned home.

The message, which I think of as a "revelation," came at a particular place and time. We were back in our home. I was alone in my study. For perhaps the thousandth time I reviewed my situation: I had had the best treatment, the best doctor; the odds had been in my favor that the disease would never return. And yet it had. Why? Did I have anything to do with it? Did I have anything to do with getting the disease in the first place? Was it a punishment? Was it a punishment I inflicted on myself? Crazy questions. Crazy thoughts. Where were they taking me?

To the image of myself hanging from a tree. A large tree overlooking the Hudson River near the home where I had grown up. Every day for weeks—no, it was months—I had thought about hanging from that tree. But that was so long ago. Years ago . . .

To explain the source of that image that I had held in my mind for those many months I must go back to my days as a schoolboy. My upbringing had been strict. My father had come to this country from Italy as a child and had worked very hard to put himself through law school. From the earliest time I can remember I was told how important education was. And so from the start I was a successful student— the top of my class. Every time I brought home an A, I was rewarded by my father with praise and money. Even though there were many students in my high school who were more intelligent than I, I managed to graduate valedictorian. I was very thin and felt physically unattractive. My entire self-esteem was based upon my success as a student. My relationship with my father was also, so it seemed to me, based upon this success. I desperately wanted my father's love and approval. Being a good student was the way I could get it.

I entered Georgetown University in the fall of 1959. It was taken for granted that after graduation I would attend law school. That is what my brother and two sisters had done (although Pat had the good sense to flunk out the first year and then pursue the career of her choice: social work). I did well at Georgetown: dean's list, mostly A's. Then I heard a lecture on psychoanalysis and it changed my life. I started reading Freud. I would study psychology, get a doctorate in clinical psychology, and become a psychotherapist. The very thought seemed heretical, a betrayal of my father, who expected his son to become a lawyer, to join him and my brother in the family practice.

Another force that was pushing me toward psychology was my mother's illness. When I was about sixteen, she became depressed. Psychiatrists had given her drugs and even electric shock treatment, but her condition was for many years unstable. I remember feeling guilty going off to college. During my freshman year I wrote my first short story, "The Man Who Cried," which was published in the college literary journal. It was about a psychotherapist who felt so deeply for his patients that he cried when he heard their sad stories. His tears seemed to heal them.

And so, yes I wanted to rescue my mother, although it never occurred to me then, but I was also intensely curious about mental illnesses and their etiology. Georgetown didn't have a program in psychology, and so I decided to transfer to Fordham after the second semester of sophomore year. I didn't dare tell my father my real reason for going to Fordham. I lied and told him that I wanted to be closer to home.

By the end of junior year at Fordham I had made up my mind about what I wanted to do with my life. I wanted to be a writer and a psychotherapist. The problem was how to tell my father. During that year and my senior year I wrote my first novel. A New York literary agent, John Schaffner, thought it publishable and it made the rounds. I applied to a number of graduate schools in clinical psychology. I had good grades—graduated *magna cum laude* and Phi Beta Kappa—and received a four-year National Institute of Mental Health fellowship to attend the University of Massachusetts. The fellowship paid not only my tuition and books, but a stipend for living expenses. Here was my chance to become independent of my father. Still, it took me months before I was able to tell him. As I expected, he was first angry, then disappointed and hurt. Why had I misled him? Why had I lied to him all these years? What was he going to do with all those wills in his office—those estates that would generate large fees? My brother Frank had just decided to leave my father's practice and strike out on his own. My father was depending on me for help. He was getting on in age; his health was failing (he was then sixty-six; at this writing he's ninety-one and still going strong). Did I know what I was doing with my life? Did I realize the risk? Psychologists did not make a lot of money. I was being foolish. I should attend law school first and then, if I still wanted to become a psychologist, I could—but with the security that I would have a real profession to fall back on.

My sisters told me to do what I wanted. My brother appeared indifferent, but signaled that he agreed with my father. Judy, my wife-to-be, the only one who knew who I was, encouraged me to stick with my decision. And I did.

The graduate program was highly competitive. We were told that no matter how well we did, a quarter of us would flunk out before the year was over. I could not face the prospect of failure and so my body rebelled. I developed all sorts of psychosomatic symptoms: gagging, tics, vomiting, and finally a spastic stomach. I was advised by the school psychiatrist that I should not give in to these symptoms but should remain in the program and do as well as I could. But I did not accept his advice. I quit before the first semester was over. It would be more accurate to say that I literally fled from the campus.

My resignation, surprisingly, did not relieve the physical symptoms, at least not for several months. Much worse than the daily vomiting and the painful stomach was the realization that the psychiatrist had been right. Failure would have been terrible, but I didn't have the courage to fail. I was a coward. My self-condemnation did not exist solely on a conscious level. Nearly every morning I would wake up and picture myself with a rope around my neck. Although I had no serious intention of committing suicide, I entertained that image of myself hanging from a tree. And not just for days or weeks, but for months.

The Recurrent Suicidal Image: What Effect Did It Have on My Immune System?

Hanging from a tree. It was such a powerful image. I made it so real. I can still see the tree in my mind's eye. I can see the very branch arching over the river's brown water where my dead body hung. The tree was opposite a small island where I had played as a boy. It was near the shore where I had seen, at age six, my first corpse—a woman who had jumped off a bridge two miles upriver. I never forgot her water-swollen body and the look of death on her face.

In recollecting the tree in the imagery, I remember how, as children, we used to swing out over the river on a thick rope tied to one of its branches. Once I lost my grip and landed on my back on the hard ground. The wind knocked out of me, I was breathless for several moments. The experience left me badly frightened. I understand now why I selected that particular tree and the rope for my suicidal visualization.

How I hated myself for quitting graduate school. How much I wanted to be dead! Had my body responded to that wish? Could it possibly be?

I struggled with that question for several days before I began to realize, began to admit that it was possible, that maybe I had predisposed myself to a life-threatening illness. I had not planned the means by which I would kill myself. But I had envisioned the end result. I had, in effect, commanded my body's defenses to surrender. And at some point in time, this is exactly what they did.

I sensed it was not merely a possibility. It was true. I felt its truth, I felt the burden of the truth, but more important I felt the power of the truth. For if I was in some way responsible for bringing on the wretched disease, then maybe I could do something about it. What? I didn't know. If the best of Western medicine had failed, I *had* to do something.

Back to the beginning. I had brought on the disease. How? With my mind. With my images. With my emotions. I had to reverse the process. With my mind. With my images. With my emotions.

How? I asked myself. How do I begin?

If I Wanted To Be Cured I Would Have To Know I Was Already Well, and Then I Would Find the Means of Survival

Then came the revelation. A voice—not external but not quite internal either—began to speak to me. The voice was clear and calm and spoke with absolute authority. It told me that if I wanted to be cured I would have to know that I was already well, and then I would find the means of survival. I tried to explain to the voice that I hadn't received the chemotherapy yet, that I couldn't possibly be cured now. But it insisted: You must *know* you are cured *now*. You mustn't doubt, you mustn't worry. You must *know*. And then, it repeated, I would find the means of survival.

The message was not rational; it was not logical. Cause preceded effect. The treatment had to precede the cure. And time! What about time? I couldn't be cured now when the treatments would come later. Forget about cause and effect, said the voice. You must know you're cured *now*. Now. With all your heart.

It seemed clear to me that I had to respond to the voice's message right then. I could not mull it over for a week or even a day. I assented and my assent was like a baptism. When I left the study, I was a different person. I was no longer ill with cancer. My life was no longer threatened. I was cured. This was a fact, something I knew. Not a wish or a hope or a belief or an expectation, but a knowing.

In the months that followed I often pictured myself walking on a tightrope a thousand feet in the air. The tightrope didn't really exist. But so long as I knew it was there, it would support me and I'd be safe. It only recently occurred to me that the hanging rope of my death imagery was transformed into the rope of my salvation.

As I bear witness to my revelation, I think it is crucial to report that in the course of the weeks, months, and years that followed, I often fell from grace. The knowing state of mind was an ideal that I strived to achieve the best I could. But there were times when worry would creep into my mind before I realized it was there. I might find myself speculating, "What would happen if I were to get still another relapse?" Then I would catch myself and respond, *That question is not admissible. I cannot admit to the possibility of becoming ill again.*

The Fear That Worrisome Thoughts Could Harm Me Was Yet Another Fear That Had To Be Dealt with and Dismissed

Whenever I became aware of worrisome thoughts, I would cast them out, as if I were exorcising devils, and would reaffirm that I was well. I would continue to be well. When the obsessive thoughts or fears would not so easily be cast aside, I would calm myself and repeat: *Negative thoughts have no influence over my body.* The fear that worry could hurt me, could perhaps initiate another recurrence, was yet another fear that had to be dealt with and dismissed. When I realized that, fearful thoughts lost their power over me. If they floated into my mind, I would escort them out. They had no power. I didn't assent to their presence. They could not harm me.

It was after the revelation that I realized I was on a healing journey. In some sense I had already arrived at my destination, since in my knowing I was already cured. And yet there were things I needed to do. The voice had promised that if I knew I was cured—if I kept that faith—I would find the means of survival. Other than the chemotherapy I was about to receive I had no idea what the voice was talking about. But I distinctly remember being ready, not to try anything that came alone, but to throw myself wholeheartedly into those special means of survival the voice said I would encounter. Somehow I would recognize what they were. That belief was another act of faith, one that I never questioned.

PART II

The Means of Survival

CHAPTER 6

The Choice: To Live or To Die

I had read about chemotherapy for the treatment of advanced Hodgkin's in one of the national news magazines. The article described the breakthrough achieved using a combination of drugs: remissions as long as three years with some of the patients. The article also described, in what I then thought was gory detail, the probable side effects of treatment: nausea, vomiting, loss of hair, suppression of the immune system. There were others.

Dr. Fischer had ascertained that Albany Medical Center had an excellent oncology clinic. For the next nine months I had to bring my body there for chemotherapy. It was not as bad as it might sound. I had to go to the clinic once every two weeks and usually was in and out in less than an hour. I was first given a blood test. Then I saw the doctor. His job was to inject a drug into a vein in my arm. The drug produced a sensation of coldness as it entered my bloodstream and began to flow through my system. It was a strange feeling, but it was not painful.

The probable side effects, in my case at least, had been exaggerated. I took three different drugs orally every day for the next week. I did have periods of nausea, but I found I could control these by always keeping something in my stomach.

The doctor never discussed the side effects with me and that was probably just as well. He did tell me to call him at any time of the

day or night if anything unusual ever occurred. I called him only
once. One evening about eleven o'clock my body began to turn red.
At first little patches of red appeared and then my entire body was
a blood-red color. I suppressed my panic long enough to telephone
the doctor at his home. He told me he had never heard of that symptom; it was most unusual. If I was still red in the morning, I should
call him.

"That was all he said?" Judy couldn't believe it.

"That was all," I replied.

So I was as red as a boiled lobster and there was nothing I could
do about it. The doctor obviously wasn't alarmed. And I remembered: *I couldn't afford to be.*

"I'm not going to worry about it," I said. "I'm going to sleep."

And I did. I woke up the next morning my usual color, but more
determined than ever to cooperate with my body, to help it get well.
After breakfast I went to my study where I could be alone. There in
the quiet, after several minutes of internal silence, a question popped
into my mind.

Do you really want to live? It seemed like a strange question. Of
course I wanted to live! I was afraid of dying, that was for sure. Afraid
of the pain, the helplessness, the humiliation, the loneliness. I had
been through all of these things, experienced them in anticipation.
No, I did not want to die.

But do you really want to live? The voice persisted. Ah, yes, I slowly
began to realize. There is a difference. I was afraid of death, a negative
emotion. But what of the positive thrust in the opposite direction?
Did I like being alive? Did I really enjoy *living?*

Oh, yes, I assured myself. I want to live. Everybody wants to live.
Don't they? This was not a time, I thought deeply, for superficial rea-
soning. This was not the time for half truths or mindless clichés. For
God's sake, for your own sake, think about it: *Do you really want to
live?*

Well, yes, in many ways. But . . . if I had to be honest there were
a lot of reasons why life was no longer attractive to me. It was very
difficult to be honest with myself. I had a wife, two sons. I loved
them deeply. And more than that: They were my responsibility. Did
I dare admit that some part of me was disappointed? Could I admit

that I might shirk my responsibility because, for reasons deep inside, I did not really want to live?

What were those reasons? Come on, I coaxed myself. You have the feeling. Let it out. It's all right. Let's go back to college. I had dreams. I had always been able to realize my dreams as a child. Oh, there were disappointments, but the big dreams somehow came true. At least that was my overall perception.

I had dreams in college. I was going to be a famous novelist. I was going to be a psychotherapist. I was going to be good at what I did. I was going to be successful.

What happened to my dreams? Gone, destroyed by reality. I had written several novels, but I was not a great novelist. I could not even get my manuscripts published. I would never be a psychotherapist. I had run away from graduate school. I was a lawyer. It was not something I wanted to be.

So now the truth. I was disappointed with my life. I was disappointed with myself. Sure, I loved my wife and children. I wanted to live for them. But what about wanting to live for myself? Yes. And No. *Ambivalence* is the word. I was ambivalent about life.

Depending upon the day, the mood, perhaps even the weather, I would have a different emotional message for my body. One day I would tell it I wanted to live; life was good, fun, enjoyable. Another day I was telling it I wanted to die; life was disappointing, I could never be all I expected to be.

And then it occurred to me: The body listens. When it receives mixed messages it reacts accordingly. A person might spend his life undulating between health and illness until one day the message that rejects life and implicitly urges death becomes predominant. Then the body's defenses begin to surrender. Then the person will have finally opted for suicide, the slow suicide of illness, disease, and death.

And that's how it is, I told myself. Now that you know the truth about yourself, what are you going to do about it? Change, change, I whispered. Let's begin by reexamining those dreams. I am not so extraordinary that I could be both a good psychotherapist and a good novelist. And there is no doubt in my mind that I would prefer to be a successful novelist. But what does it mean to be a successful novelist? Does it mean that I must be famous? No, not necessarily. It means that I have to be able to write good novels. I know I have some talent. Now I need to learn the craft. Now I have to learn discipline. Writing novels was easy for me. Too easy. Simply writing novels does not make one a good novelist. I have to study the form. I have to become an apprentice, then a journeyman. Perhaps never a master. But that's not important. What is important is that I learn to write good novels. I know it is terribly difficult to accomplish. But I can do it. With patience and hard work, I can.

Reclaim your dreams, I told myself. Reclaim your dreams. My commitment to life, I realized, was based in part on attempting to fulfill my dreams.

Testing My Commitment to Life on a Physical Level

I had made an intellectual commitment to life. I had examined the inner chambers of heart and mind, had found the truth about my ambivalence, and had opted for *living*. But was it enough? For some reason, I wanted to feel the decision on a physical level. I wanted to make a physical choice for life. I wanted to test my commitment.

I had always been fearful of flying. I had been a passenger on a commercial airline when I was about fifteen and after that when I was seventeen. Both times I was terrified. I was certain that the plane would crash.

When I was nearly eighteen, my brother had the opportunity to take free flying lessons in a single-engine plane. But he decided he didn't have the time and he passed the opportunity on to me. It was not something I wanted to do, but I did not dare admit to him I was afraid. And so I took about fifteen hours of instruction and made my first solo flight. It was an exciting, but overall an unpleasant, experience.

I remember the day the instructor signed my certificate and said I was ready to fly alone. He warned me not to stay up too long because winds might be building up. The takeoff was flawless and then I broke pattern and flew for about a half hour in the vicinity of the airport. The most difficult part of flying is landing the airplane, and it was with trepidation that I reentered the landing pattern of the field and made my approach to the runway.

I did everything I had done when the instructor had been present. I seemed to be at the right altitude and was flying at the proper airspeed. I was gliding slowly toward the runway. But instead of the plane settling at the beginning of the runway as I had expected, it flew on until I was nearly halfway down the runway. The runway was a small grass strip, and in order to land safely you had to land at the beginning of the field. I realized I had to abort the landing and I quickly applied full throttle. The plane's engine roared and I slowly climbed back into the sky.

I remained in the pattern of the airport and once again made my approach. I tried to understand why the plane had come in high but was unable to figure out what I had done wrong. The result was that on the second approach I did exactly what I had done the first time. I was nearly halfway down the field before I was ready to land and by then it was too late. I forced in the throttle and climbed out. As I ascended I noticed that my instructor and some other people had come out of the small terminal office and were standing in a group about fifty feet from the runway. Don't worry, I thought. Don't worry, I told myself. I'll make it this time.

I was determined to land within the first ten feet of the runway. The problem was I could not come down too quickly because there was a fence in front of the landing strip. On my third approach I was careful to place my nose wheel down at the beginning of the runway, but I had made another mistake: I had not monitored my airspeed and I came in much too fast. The nose wheel hit the ground and then bumped off the earth's surface. I attempted to place the plane in the right landing attitude by pulling back on the stick. The plane began to settle down toward the ground, but once again I was approaching the middle of the landing field. If I landed the plane, I would not have enough runway left to stop it, and I'd end up in the small lake at the end of the field. For the third time, I pushed the throttle in as far as it would go, released my flaps, and listened for the reassuring sound of the engine's roar. But instead of roaring, it choked and sputtered and the plane began to fall. My heart seemed to drop faster than the plane, but then the engine caught and I was on my way up.

It has to be this time, I thought on my fourth approach. The landing was not a good one; it was bouncy, but I hardly cared. I was down. And I made a quiet but firm resolve to *stay down*.

It was nearly twelve years later, when I was sitting in my study thinking about the need to physically test my commitment to life, that I thought about flying again. It was the perfect vehicle! For flying involves life or death decisions. On takeoffs or landings, it would be very easy to make a "mistake," especially when trying to adjust to a crosswind or a sudden gust of wind. Look, I told myself, like it or not, you're going to learn to fly again. This time you're going to get your pilot's license. If you want to kill yourself, you'll have plenty of opportunities. If you want to live, you'll have the chance to prove it.

I began taking lessons in the late spring of 1971 and had my license by September. It took me longer than it should have because I was receiving chemotherapy during this period. FAA regulations prohibited me from flying whenever I had any drugs in my system. About two weeks a month I was off drugs and it was during those periods that I flew.

When I remember what I wanted my flying to accomplish, one event remains vivid in my mind. It was a fairly windy day but still safe for me to fly since I had been up in windy conditions with my instructor. I took off without incident but as soon as the plane was a hundred feet off the ground (and as I was approaching the lake) a sudden gust of wind literally pushed the plane to the right, raising the left wing. The wind force was quite sustained and I fought to keep the plane from turning over and diving into the ground. It was a thrilling, exhilarating moment because I knew that I was fighting for my life. I can see myself even now forcing the stick to the left, pressing hard on the left rudder, dropping the nose of the plane to reduce the chances of the plane stalling. The plane responded and with me fought its way out of the torrent of wind.

I had another frightening experience when I was on my first solo cross-country flight. I was to fly to another airport about one hundred miles away. En route, I realized that I was alone thousands of feet up in the air inside a tiny compartment a few feet wide, a few feet long. The engine hummed on monotonously, and though I was traveling at about 120 miles per hour, it seemed like I was going nowhere. How much I wanted to stop the engine and get out! Right then, right there! I couldn't stand to be in that tiny capsule for another second. Where was I going? What was I doing up here? Was it ever going to end? And if it was, wouldn't it be better if it ended now?

Patience, I told myself. I have a destination. It's only forty minutes away. *But time is nothing. A minute is eternity.* That's all right. Patience.

I finally saw the airport and landed the plane safely. I found one of the local flight instructors and had him sign my book as proof that I had completed the flight. Then I walked into the coffee shop and lingered for a long time over a cup of coffee. I hardly understood my fears. No, I really didn't want to fly the airplane back home. I wanted to call my instructor and tell him I was through with flying forever.

When We Face Our Fears—Even the Fear of Death—They Begin To Lose Power Over Us

I continued to sit thinking about my fear, the fear of dying. For some reason, if I didn't think about it, if I didn't face it, the fear acquired more power over me. It was the same with other fears: of failure, of disappointment, of boredom and monotony, of the emptiness that came from thinking my life was meaningless. I resolved to try to be aware of my fears. How easy it was to bury them, to let the crust of everyday, of routine, adhere to me like a mold and make me insensitive to what was inside. I could no longer afford to be sad or disappointed, even on the inside. *Especially* on the inside. As for the fear, the ultimate fear, what could be done about that? I didn't know, but I sensed that if I reached outward toward it, if I tried to push against it, then the fear of death, even death itself, would lose its strength.

With these thoughts I got back into the plane for the flight back home. It was an easy trip and I felt good being up there alone.

My early flying experience was a battlefield I created on which I could fight for my life. I was in some mystical sense a warrior and Death was my adversary.

The following spring I bought a motorcycle. Driving it, often at excessive speeds, became yet another battlefield on which I challenged Death. It wasn't an intelligent thing to do; risking my life was foolish. It was my primitive way of engaging Death. Taunting it. I remember thinking more than once as I sped along a country road, "Death, I'm not afraid of you. I've come out to meet you. Catch me. Catch me if you can."

My message to Death—and obviously to myself—was: I will fight for my life with every resource I have—with my mind, with my spirit, with my body, with my heart. I will fight as hard as I can.

I flew and rode my motorcycle on and off for three years. When these tools which I had fashioned to express my fighting spirit were no longer needed, I discarded them.

Flying and riding a motorcycle made me acutely aware of how sacred life is—and how easily it can be lost. It gave me the opportunity to embrace life, to seize it with my hands, to guard it, knowing it's the most precious thing there is. To this day all of life continues to be a great mystery to me, a great gift, even in its so-called lower forms. If I find an insect in the house—a moth, a bee, a spider—I catch it and carry it outside. How could I destroy what I am unable to restore?

CHAPTER 7

Means of Survival: Meditation

There was one emotion I had great difficulty dealing with at the oncology clinic: rage. The more I went the worse it seemed to get. At times I felt I wanted to "go crazy"—whatever that meant. Maybe smash the doctor in the face. Dump over the magazine rack in the waiting area. Rip up the magazines. At other times I wanted to kill.

There was always a crowd of us waiting. First we would check in with the receptionist, then wait for as long as an hour to be called. I hated to have my name called aloud, and I sat in dread waiting for it to happen. I often sneaked glances at other cancer patients. Some were young. Maybe they had a chance. I *knew* I had a chance. I *knew* I was going to beat it. But some of the old ones were gray-faced. Even some not so old, in their forties, fifties. I sensed the gray-faced ones were as good as dead. I can still picture some of their faces—always thin, eyes looking inside, not out.

I Dealt with My Rage by Making My Mind Go Blank

God, how I hated being there. I often fought the rage by making my mind dead. I refused to think. I would stare at objects, count the beat

71

of time, sometimes pace back and forth in the waiting room. I would never touch a magazine. I would never read. I didn't want to leave so much as a fingerprint of mine in that room, and I would never bring anything with me, such as a book, that would remind me of the place when I got back home.

The visits to the clinic were not a part of my life. They were something else. It was almost as if a different person was going inside the hospital to the clinic to wait for his name—not mine—to be yelled out by the unthinking nurse. A different person contained his rage, refused to go berserk. A different person was shot up with the cold liquid and given a week's supply of pills. And then when I got outside the walls, I was me again.

Even now, years later, when forced as I am at this moment to think of myself sitting in the waiting room, I remember the rage. And how it often made me want to go mad, to destroy every semblance of order in sight. Dishes should be smashed, chairs should be broken, lamps crushed, rugs ripped, people stabbed. Why keep the façade of sanity outside when in there—in the clinic room—life is upside down, absurd, insane?

It was December 1971. The chemotherapy was over. I had tolerated the full dosage. I was told to return in three months for a checkup.

Late one Sunday evening the telephone rang. It was my brother. "I just got back from New York," he said. "I have to tell you about the course. I'll be right over."

The "course" he was referring to was Silva Mind Control, which he had just completed. He had gone to New York City the weekend before to begin the four-day seminar. He had told me a little about the first two days: "conditioning"; alpha brain waves; "programming"; visualization. I was not terribly impressed. His instructor had told the class that on the final day they would experience extrasensory perception or something similar to it, but even my brother was skeptical. He had never experienced psychic phenomena before and did not believe it was possible.

When he arrived, he told me exactly what it was he had experienced. He had been told that one of the things he could do in a deep state of relaxation, in "alpha," was to "tune in" to another person to make a psychic determination of that person's physical condition and then, by visualization and other techniques, to correct any malady. In other words, psychic diagnosis and psychic healing! Toward the end of the fourth day of class, the students had been instructed to form groups of three. Each person was told to write down on a card the name of a person, a brief physical description, and the person's sex, age, and city, together with any ailments the person had. One person in the group then went down to his "level," down to alpha, and was given simply the name, sex, age, and city of the person. He was then told to freely report what he "saw" or felt about the person.

My brother reported that everyone in the class experienced success. He had submitted my father's name and the student was correctly able to diagnose my father's major medical problems, which included an aneurysm on the back of his left knee. Most important (and this was the part of the story my brother was building up to), he had given another student *my* name and the student had correctly reported that I had a disease of the lymph system! The student said he could "see" my kidneys and my liver fighting to rid the body of its impurities, and that he could also "see" that my body would succeed in overcoming the illness. He suggested that I do more physical exercise.

Of course I was quite happy to hear the amateur psychic's hopeful prognosis. Although at this point in my life I had already stamped firmly in my consciousness the affirmation that I was healed, still it was beneficial to receive outside confirmation.

I asked my brother if he had been able to psychically detect illness, and he said yes. He was not able to "see" or to "feel" the illness as other students could, but when he tuned into the subject he was working on, he suddenly was aware of information about the person. He began to talk about the person, and most of what he said was accurate.

My brother urged me to take the course as soon as possible, and I agreed to do so. I believed that my brother was attempting to report accurately what he had observed, but I did not really think these strange phenomena had actually occurred. Perhaps there had been a lucky guess here and there, but what he had purported to observe was simply too incredible. However, my curiosity was sufficiently aroused to invest four days of my time as well as the tuition fee of $150.

On the first Saturday morning, I found myself in a class of fifteen people, ranging in age from about sixteen to seventy. There were also several "graduates" who had come to review various parts of the course. (Graduates are allowed to repeat the course as frequently as they wish, free of charge.)

Silva Mind Control begins with the old cliché that man uses only about 10 percent of his brain. It then goes on to teach you how to use a good percentage of the remainder.

It was explained that when we are awake, we are generally in the beta brain frequency. When we are asleep and dreaming, we are generally in alpha. While sleeping, we may also be in theta or in delta. In theta, we are oblivious to pain, while in the deeper delta state we are totally unconscious. Silva Mind Control says that we can learn to go into alpha and even theta while remaining conscious. This means we are able to consciously control the things that generally happen only in these states.

Relaxed, somewhat content, and fully convinced that the instructor is a con man, I am ready for the first "conditioning." We are encouraged to lie on the floor and become completely relaxed. The first conditioning takes perhaps thirty minutes. We are taught to relax each part of the body and then to relax the mind. A number from six to one is assigned to each part of the process, and an association is built between that number and a particular relaxed state of body and mind. Before the course is over, by imagining and saying only the numbers, one is able to enter alpha in a few seconds.

Alpha is not a single state of mind but a level or range. At the end of the first conditioning, the longest, I began to dream, although I was also conscious of what the instructor was saying. During the shorter conditionings I did not dream, but I often became completely unaware of my body; it seemed to have drifted away. Most people were never quite sure during the course whether they were in alpha or not; the instructor simply assured them that they were.

During the first three days, we practiced the conditionings, which became shorter and shorter. We were taught how to use the alpha state in various ways: to control weight; to remember dreams; to program ourselves to remember what we read; to find solutions to problems; to control headache and other pain; to control sleep and wakefulness.

At the end of the second day and during the third day, while in alpha, we began to project ourselves (with our newly trained imaginations) into inanimate objects, into plants, into animals, and finally into people. We were told *nothing is impossible*. Our minds can travel to any place in the universe; we can gather information there. Our brains emit energy which can influence other people (always for the better), and which can make people become healthy if they are ill! This is the kingdom within; this is where Jesus spent much of his time. But it is a state *natural* to all people if they could only learn to use it, if they would only have faith that these powers are theirs for the asking.

We are told these things and perhaps some of us begin to believe them. If, for three days, someone persistently insists you are a genius, after a while you stop arguing that you are not. Extrasensory perception? Why not! And perhaps that is why it works.

On the final day, the students broke up into groups of three. Each of us had written down on a piece of paper the names of several people with their age, sex, city, a physical description, and anything we knew about the person's health. I first observed others close their eyes and then, when given only the name, age, sex, and city, begin to describe the person and his physical problems with uncanny accuracy.

After Performing Psychic Diagnosis I Was No Longer Sure If I Was a Man or Some Kind of God

When it came my turn to perform, while I was fully aware that what I was attempting was insane, I closed my eyes, went into alpha, and was given the name of a man in a neighboring town—a person I had never heard of before. In my mind, I saw the man. I said, "Yes, I see him. He is partially bald and has white hair. He is wearing glasses, not regular ones but metal ones, and he has a bulbous-shaped nose." The person who submitted his name (a New York State trooper) responded, "That's exactly what he looks like." I then scanned the body in my mind. I was attracted to his hands, his feet, and then to his pelvic area. I focused on his hands. They were swollen and the bones were a luminescent white. The feet were similar. I saw the same glowing whiteness on his pelvic bone. Then the word *arthritis* came to mind. I said, "He has arthritis of the hands, feet, and pelvic bone. His hands and feet are swollen." While I held the man in view, I attempted to help his condition by visualizing the swelling going down and the whiteness becoming less intense. The trooper later told me I had described the man's condition accurately.

I did many other "cases" that day with the same accuracy. Each time the name, sex, age, and city of the person were given to me, a vivid picture of the person formed in my mind. I saw one woman as being depressed and saw that she had had a hysterectomy. I saw another woman in the hospital with a lung condition. I was given the name of a man who lived in the Midwest. As I scanned his body, I saw his throat was black. I reported that he had cancer of the throat and I was right. One of the more interesting cases was a woman from Miami, Florida. When I was given her name, I saw a caricature of a short, fat woman. She was talking while I pictured her, and as long as I held the image, she did not stop talking. When I mentioned this the woman who submitted her name said, "That is her, all right. She never shuts up." I felt the woman had a digestive problem caused by her overeating, and I reported this intuition. I was told that I was correct, but that there was also another problem. I continued to scan the woman's body, but did not see anything else. At this time, I let my hands relax in front of me and I said, "Well, whatever it is, I can't find it." As soon as I said that, I "saw" superimposed over my hands two fat little hands. They were quite swollen. Then I had an image of the hands wearing turquoise rubber gloves. I also saw that the feet were swollen. There was no special whiteness about the swelling so I knew it was not arthritis. I reported what I had seen. "Yes," I was told. "She's allergic to something and it causes her hands and feet to swell. Water aggravates the condition and that's why she always wears rubber gloves when she puts her hands in water."

Silva Mind Control does not try to explain why these and similar phenomena occur. During the breaks, the instructor and interested students and graduates will talk about Jung's collective unconscious, Alan Watts, some of the Eastern philosophies and religions, Edgar Cayce and other psychics. But Silva Mind Control is primarily interested in teaching the method by which people may achieve . . . anything.

At the time I took Silva Mind Control, I was not interested in psychic diagnosis or psychic healing. I was interested in self-healing. The instructor suggested that people with specific problems meditate three times a day for about fifteen minutes. For the first couple of years after taking the course, I maintained this regimen, but thereafter became less rigid about the schedule and meditated when I felt the need to do so. I usually meditate at least once a day, sometimes for a few minutes, other times for as long as an hour.

I begin my meditation by becoming very relaxed. I usually turn the lights out and lie down. I enter my "level" by counting and visualizing the numbers 3, 2, and 1, three times each in succession. These numbers are associated with physical relaxation, mental relaxation, and total relaxation, respectively; mind control graduates are conditioned to relax deeply when these numbers are visualized. To enter into a deeper state of relaxation, I count slowly, from ten to one, imagining the numbers at the same time. I try to feel that I am going deeper, and it sometimes helps to imagine that I am walking down a flight of stairs. I clear my mind of all thought and try to feel an inner silence and peace.

When I do this exercise, my subjective states are quite variable. Sometimes I go quite deep and fall off to sleep. Other times my body seems to fall asleep but my mind remains active. I no longer feel my body, but I am conscious. Sometimes I lose consciousness, yet I am not asleep. If someone walks into the room, I will hear him. If I am spoken to, I am able to respond. But when there is no stimulus, I become unaware. I am neither thinking nor feeling.

When I Am in a State of Deep Relaxation I Program My Body To Be Well

Most of the time, however, I am simply relaxed. When I feel as deeply relaxed as I can be, I begin to "program" my body. I do this by verbal affirmations and by visual images. For example, I think: "I am and I will continue to be in a state of perfect health. I am whole, I am pure, I am in balance." One of the affirmations suggested in the mind control course is, "I will never learn to develop physically or mentally, mentally or physically, the symptoms or any of the conditions of the disease known as cancer." One can, of course, add to the number of diseases, and I usually include a number of specific diseases which I tell myself I will avoid.

I then visualize myself looking very robust and happy. I verbally affirm that certain organs in my body are whole and, at the same time, I visualize these organs looking that way. Thus I often "see" my lungs, heart, liver, and kidneys in a healthy state, and then I go on to affirm the well-being of my blood, my lymph system, and my skin. I sometimes imagine my lymph system looking healthy. I scan my body and visualize the lymphatic vessels and tiny nodes looking white and pure. Sometimes I visualize my immune system as glittering atoms of energy throughout my body, poised to strike and destroy any foreign element or cell that is injurious to my body.

Following the advice I received from my mind control instructor, I place no limitations on my imagination. Each graduate, for example, has imagined "counselors" who exist in an imagined laboratory. I often go to my laboratory where my counselors work on my body. One Chinese counselor uses acupuncture; another brings me an orange solution which I drink. Sometimes they affirm and repeat that I am well and in perfect health.

Another technique I use is to ask my "brothers and sisters" throughout the universe to send me their healing thoughts, prayers, and graces that I may maintain myself in a state of perfect health. While saying this, I often picture particular people who I feel are filled with love and compassion.

In addition to meditations during the day, I try to program myself just before, during, and immediately after sleep. Just before falling asleep, I think of one or two affirmations of health. If I awaken during the night, I will try to repeat the affirmations. What I am attempting to do is to reach the subconscious parts of my mind, and these parts are more open during these periods.

Silva Mind Control was my introduction to meditation. It is a meditative technique in that it teaches you how to focus the mind on a thought such as an affirmation or an image and to hold it there for long periods. This particular type of meditation, with its emphasis on affirmations and visualizations, was extremely important in my own self-healing. It was the foundation for all that was to follow.

The practice of meditation also helped me to deal with strong emotions, such as the rage I had experienced in the oncology clinic. Daily meditation helped me to become more serene.

When I entered the new year, 1972, I had a new tool. There *was* a way I could help myself. Positive thoughts, positive images. I would never again picture myself hanging from a tree. Instead I would "see" myself as strong and healthy. I would try to give my body only one message, the message of life.

CHAPTER 8

Means of Survival: The Edgar Cayce Readings

Years before I had been introduced to Silva Mind Control, I had read a book about a fascinating man, Edgar Cayce. Once again, the recommendation came from my brother. The book was *The Sleeping Prophet* by Jess Stern. Like so many others, I was intrigued by Cayce's life, but I had no idea at that time that Cayce would have such a direct and profound effect upon my own life.

Edgar Cayce was an American psychic who died in 1945. He was born in Hopkinsville, Kentucky, in 1877 and led a normal childhood except for a vision he had when he was seven years old. In the vision he was asked what he wanted to do with his life. He said simply that he wanted to help others, especially children. He was told his prayers had been answered. It was not until seventeen years later that anything remarkable occurred. Cayce had lost his voice and a cure was attempted through hypnotic suggestion. The young Cayce discovered that he could go to sleep and answer questions put to him. He himself never heard a word said, nor did he remember anything when he woke up. For the next forty-three years, Cayce lay down and entered his sleep state at least twice a day.

Numerous books have been written about him and the many topics he discussed while in a trancelike state. One of the most important things he did was to give medical readings to people with various diseases. Between 1910 and 1945, he gave nearly nine thousand medical readings. Fortunately, everything he said during these readings was recorded by his secretary, Gladys Davis. The readings have been indexed according to subject matter by the foundation that carries on his work, the Association for Research and Enlightenment, in Virginia Beach, Virginia. They are available free of charge to members of the association.

While awake, Edgar Cayce had flashes of insight and manifested some psychic abilities. When asleep, however, he was able to obtain information that he said came from universal sources. He was able to describe events in the future as well as discuss the physiological functioning of a sick person who might be thousands of miles away. It has been said that in this state he was able to communicate with the unconscious minds of people everywhere and specifically with the mind of the person for whom he was giving the reading.

I had thought about sending for the A.R.E. file on Hodgkin's disease for over a year. For some reason I didn't want to do so until the chemotherapy was finished. Now that the regular treatment was over, I felt free—and compelled—to pursue other remedies.

As much as I had hated the trips to the clinic, I felt a kind of security being under the doctor's supervision and receiving the chemicals that I knew were deadly to any diseased cells that might be in my body. But now my body was on its own; it had to rely—I had to rely—on its own natural defenses. I had found one means of survival: meditation. I had to find others.

Although Cayce's Readings Were Difficult to Comprehend, There Was Sufficient Information to Form a Treatment Plan

The file I received contained the four readings Cayce had done for people diagnosed with Hodgkin's. I was initially disappointed with the materials because Cayce's explanation for the disease was incomprehensible to me. Moreover, the suggested treatments varied from case to case. Nevertheless, I decided to extract from the file a prescription that I could apply to myself.

One reading that was particularly clear gave the following advice:

> "First, let's give that as may aid in relieving the tensions: One hour each day for three days in succession, apply hot castor oil packs across the abdominal area and entirely around the body—that is, over the abdominal as well as the back area. Apply these as warm as the body can well stand. This may give a little distress at the first period. Afterward there will be much ease. After taking the third pack, on the evening of the third day, you see,—take internally three tablespoonfuls of pure olive oil. After resting a day following the series of the castor oil packs, begin with osteopathic adjustments with special reference to the coccyx centers and the 6th and 7th dorsal center. Do not attempt to make all adjustments necessary at one time, but have a series of treatments to gradually make adjustment."

Cayce recommended that the three-day series of castor oil packs be repeated in about ten days or two weeks and that they be continued at these intervals "until there has been the adjusting of the pressures in the coccyx and the upper dorsal areas, and until the rest of the cerebrospinal system is coordinated." He also suggested periodic colonics.

After analyzing the four readings, I decided to use several of the Cayce treatments: the castor oil packs, the osteopathic adjustments, and the ingestion of a drug called atomidine, which is 1 percent nascent iodine.

I soon found that the purchase of castor oil in retail stores in the quantity needed to soak pieces of cloth was quite expensive. I therefore began purchasing castor oil by the gallon from a chemical wholesaler. I used some old diapers for the cloth and soaked them in the oil, which I had heated on the stove. By trial and error, I found that I could not heat the oil very long before it would begin to smoke and quickly fill the house with fumes. More than once I made the house stink for days, and Judy was not happy about it. I carried the "rags," as I called them, to my bedroom in a metal pan and then prepared the bed first with a large towel and then with plastic wrap. I placed one rag on the plastic wrap, and when it had cooled enough for me to stand it, I lay down on my back. I then placed the other rag over the abdominal area and securely wrapped myself in the plastic wrap so that there would be no leakage. Finally I placed a heating pad over my stomach and then lay back to enjoy it.

Judy hadn't read the Cayce materials and certainly was not a believer in Cayce's miraculous powers. Her attitude was, Who knows? It might help so it's worth trying. She often assisted me in preparing the castor oil packs and in arranging the bed to prevent the oil from seeping into the mattress.

Cayce Emphasized That a Positive Attitude Is Most Important in Healing

Sometimes when I was "in oils," I meditated; other times I read. I found it a relaxing experience. I tried to remember during these periods that Cayce emphasized again and again that attitude is most important in healing—that ultimately all healing must come from within. He said that all treatments should be combined with the prayerful, expectant use of abilities and strength. "Keep up mental and spiritual attitude of being good for something. Let all ye do be with a purpose founded in spiritual concepts. Keep mental attitude creative."

After one to two hours I would remove the oil with paper tissue. The next day my bowels would be unusually soft, indicating that the oil had entered my system.

The selection of an osteopathic physician in Albany was not difficult; there was only one, Dr. John Pike. I called his secretary and made an appointment. When she asked what the problem was, I muttered, "My back." I felt sheepish about explaining my real purpose. Dr. Pike's office adjoined his house in a suburb of Albany. On the way there, I racked my brain, trying to figure out a way of making my outlandish request—that he treat me according to the guidelines set forth by a simple uneducated man who had been dead over thirty years.

Dr. Pike was a kindly old gentleman with silver hair and intelligent, sensitive eyes. He listened carefully as I told him my medical history. Finally I told him about Edgar Cayce and how I felt a little foolish about what I was asking him to do. At the mention of Cayce's name, Dr. Pike smiled and I knew he had a secret. "I don't share this with everyone," he said. Then he told me: "In 1938 a woman walked into my office. It was then in downtown Albany on State Street. She told me she had just returned from Virginia Beach where she had a psychic reading from Edgar Cayce." Dr. Pike shook his head as he recalled his meeting with this patient. "I never heard of this fellow. She explained who he was and then—this will really get you—she told me that Cayce had described to her the person who could treat her in her hometown, Albany. Me! He described me! Can you imagine? And where my office was." Dr. Pike shook his head again, as if it was still difficult for him to believe. "Well, I treated her, and since that time hundreds more have been sent by Edgar Cayce. In a way, you are his latest referral."

For several years I went to Dr. Pike's office for osteopathic adjustments about twice a week. As Cayce suggested, I scheduled treatments in a series, first for about sixteen weeks, and then a rest period of about eight weeks, then eight weeks of treatments and a rest of four weeks, and so forth.

During this time I took atomidine, as prescribed by Cayce: one drop in a glass of water on the morning of the first day, two drops the second day, and so on until five drops had been taken. Then I abstained for two days and began again. Sometimes I discontinued the drops for a week.

The Cayce readings were enthusiastic about the use of atomidine in cases involving glandular deficiency or malfunction, recommending it for a wide range of illnesses. Cayce said it could be used whenever there was an indication of an unbalancing of either glandular activity or the assimilating and eliminating system activity. He emphasized that it was not only a curative property, but a preventive. Since each drop of atomidine supplies approximately six times the minimum daily requirement of iodine, in a few of the readings Cayce warned about taking too much atomidine when the person was getting iodine from other sources.

In late 1972 I decided to correspond with the director of the A.R.E. Clinic in Phoenix, Arizona, to ask if I was properly following the suggestions in the file. I received a quick reply from Dr. William A. McGarey, who, with his wife Gladys, also a medical doctor, and several other physicians, operated the clinic. In addition to the methods of treatment I was using, Dr. McGarey said that patients at his clinic also used a wet cell battery device and several times a day inhaled the fumes from apple brandy that had been placed in a charred oaken keg. I added these procedures to the other Cayce remedies, which I continued to use regularly for the next three years. After that time, I felt I no longer needed the treatments. They had accomplished their purpose.

Cayce's Theories Seemed to Have Some Scientific Basis

Although I had never been concerned with finding scientific proof to support Cayce's formulas, it was heartening to read a report, authored by Dr. McGarey, in a monthly medical research bulletin. He mentioned a recent finding that patients with Hodgkin's disease have low blood levels of thymosin, a hormone produced by the thymus gland. The thymus is the master gland of the immune system and it has been known for some time that cells from this gland migrate to other portions of the body and become centers of lymphatic activity. Dr. McGarey pointed out that Cayce attributed great importance to the Peyer's patches—a series of lymph nodules in the lining of the small intestine. Cayce had said that regular use of castor oil packs over the abdomen would help the lymphatic system regain its integrity to function. Dr. McGarey speculated that it was likely that the secretions produced by the Peyer's patches contain thymosin.

One concept repeated again and again in the Cayce readings is the necessity of maintaining "balance" within the body. Cayce described the life force which flows through the body in the manner of a figure eight and said that the right vibrations tuned into this flow would equalize deficient or superfluous energy charges on various organs or portions of the body. *Balance* was a word I responded to on almost a visceral level. Just saying it was soothing. I remember it was an important element of Greek philosophy. The word led me to my next means of survival.

CHAPTER 9

Means of Survival: Acupuncture

I n the early 1970s the first articles about acupuncture appeared in the American press. One of the more in-depth articles discussed the underlying philosophy of acupuncture—the restoration and maintenance of *balance* of life energy called "ch'i."

Although some of the articles stated that acupuncture could not be used to treat cancer, I decided to research the subject and read several books on acupuncture. Acupuncture is based on the premise that any disease has two main phases, the invisible and the visible. The first represents an energy imbalance or disturbance before it has shown itself in the body tissues or processes as symptoms. The highest art of the traditional acupuncture practitioner is to treat the energy imbalance at that point to *prevent* the disease from ever occurring. The second phase of a disturbed energy balance comes when the unchecked first-stage imbalance begins to manifest itself in outward symptoms. When acupuncture was used five thousand years ago, a good doctor was paid only if his patients did not develop disease. If symptoms did appear, he was not paid for his treatments. Thus the Chinese proverb: "The superior doctor prevents illness; the mediocre doctor cures imminent illness; the inferior doctor treats actual illness."

I Decided To Try Acupuncture To Get My Body in Balance

After pondering the books I had read, I decided to be treated with acupuncture. My theory was that the radiation and chemotherapy may well have killed all the disease in my body, but what about the cause of the disease? If my body was not corrected or adjusted in some significant way, what was to prevent it from occurring again? Of course, there was meditation and the Cayce applications, but why stop there? Here was another tool, and I would use it.

The search for a competent acupuncturist began. I could find no information about practitioners in the United States, although I was sure they existed in New York City and San Francisco. Then I learned of Dr. Y. C. Siow through a friend who saw him on NBC's "First Tuesday." I obtained his address from the station and wrote to him in London. My letter was quite detailed, several pages single-spaced. I thought it was important that he have a complete history so that he could determine whether he could help me. The response was disheartening. It stated, "Your case is quite difficult to treat. It can be helped by acupuncture treatment but it takes time to have complete recovery. It depends upon individual responses which I am unable to predict. . . . There is always hope to be cured by this kind of treatment."

The reason I was disheartened was because the response was contained in a form letter. Did he even read my letter? Perhaps he was too busy. After all, the television special about him indicated he was quite famous in Europe. He had cured Prince Bernhard of Holland of a back condition, and the Dutch flocked to London to see him.

I decided to write to another British acupuncturist, Dr. Felix Mann. He was the author of several books about acupuncture and headed the British Acupuncture Society, a group of medical doctors who practice acupuncture in England. Dr. Siow had attended medical school in China and had served a long clinical internship in his father's clinic in Singapore, but he was not considered a medical doctor in the West.

Dr. Mann's response was frankly discouraging. While he did not advise against treatment, he said that he did not treat cancer patients with acupuncture except to control pain. He suggested that I have my doctor telephone him in London.

I had discussed with Dr. Fischer the possibility of my going to London for treatment and had asked him if he would accompany me. I explained I was afraid of the acupuncture needles, and I would feel better if he were there to make sure the acupuncturist did nothing to harm me. He neither encouraged nor discouraged me but said that if I decided to go, he would come along as an observer. He made the telephone call to Dr. Mann, and Dr. Mann repeated what he had told me in the letter. He said, however, that he might be inclined to treat me if I wanted him to.

During this period some American physicians were becoming interested in acupuncture, at least as an anesthetic. I read in the *New York Times* that Dr. John Fox, an anesthesiologist from Downstate Medical College in Brooklyn, was the sponsor of an acupuncture symposium. I wrote to Dr. Fox and asked if, in his opinion, acupuncture could treat Hodgkin's. I received a mimeographed letter which answered my question. "According to medical texts on acupuncture and what I understand of it, these diseases or conditions are *not* helped by acupuncture: cancer, leukemias, Hodgkin's disease, paralysis from spinal cord injury, mental illnesses, multiple sclerosis, sickle cell anemia, mongolism, drug abuse, drug addiction, alcoholism, diabetes, birth defects or birth injuries, cerebral palsy. The above diseases or conditions are *not* helped by acupuncture." Dr. Fox then cited four reference books that those seeking further information might find helpful. Interestingly enough, none of the books he recommended had been written by an Asian.

Fortunately, I did not believe that the written word of a physician, even an American physician, was absolute truth. I had read that many of the diseases he claimed were untreatable were in fact ameliorated with acupuncture. It was clear that we had not read the same books. Dr. Fox's response provided me with the first inkling that a Western physician's interpretation and application of acupuncture is apt to be much different from that of a physician educated in the East. Dr. Fox's mentor in this area had been Dr. Mann, and even Dr. Mann had thought of acupuncture as a tool to be used as an adjunct to Western medicine and not as a system of medicine in its own right. It occurred to me that if I were to benefit from acupuncture, I probably should be treated by someone who considered it a complete and primary treatment rather than merely an adjunct.

I wrote to Dr. Siow and asked him if I could see him during a certain week in May. He replied that he would be available. I also arranged to see Dr. Mann that same week. Dr. Fischer and I arrived in London on a Saturday morning late in May.

In the Chinese System, I Had a Deficiency of Ch'i Energy in the Liver

On Monday morning we went to Dr. Mann's office. After a brief discussion with Dr. Fischer, Dr. Mann took my pulses, the main diagnostic procedure in the Chinese system. Pulse diagnosis requires feeling not one but twelve different pulses in the arteries of the wrists. Each pulse corresponds to a particular organ or function within the Chinese system. Pulse diagnosis is an art in itself, since a skilled diagnostician can differentiate up to twenty-seven different qualities in the pulses. A pulse, for example, will not be felt simply as strong or weak, but it may be "slippery" or "wet" or "brittle." After feeling the pulses on both my wrists, Dr. Mann made his diagnosis: I had a deficiency of ch'i energy in my liver. He said he would be willing to correct the condition but did not know if it would be helpful in preventing a recurrence of cancer. I thanked him for his time and opinion and said I would think about what he had told us. I was eager to get to our afternoon appointment with Dr. Siow.

Dr. Siow lived in Wembley, a village just outside of London, about a thirty-minute ride by underground from our hotel. When we entered his office—a converted garage adjoining his house—several people were sitting in the waiting room. The furniture was quite modest, even a bit uncomfortable.

After a few minutes Dr. Siow, dressed in a black suit, opened a door, smiled to everyone, and called the name of the patient who was next. He was much younger than I had expected, about thirty-eight. When my turn came, he greeted Dr. Fischer and me warmly. Dr. Siow asked me to tell him about my condition. As I told him my medical history, he observed me carefully, especially my face. He asked if I slept well and about my health in general. Did I feel well? Was my general level of energy and activity satisfactory? Dr. Siow commented that I was quite thin and asked if this was my normal body structure. There were also more specific questions about the patterns and amount of urine passed and about appetite. As we talked he held first one wrist and then the other, and I knew he was feeling my pulses. Then he took my blood pressure. Abruptly, he said he would begin treatment now and asked me to remove all my clothes except my underwear. I was somewhat startled, but I no longer feared the treatment for I had read that the needles did not hurt. I was to learn otherwise. Before treatment began I asked Dr. Siow what he had found from the pulse diagnosis. His reply: "You have a deficiency of ch'i energy in the liver."

I sat in a chair facing a small flower garden. I tried to relax as much as possible. Dr. Siow first dabbed the skin with alcohol and then made the insertions. The depth of the insertions varied from just beneath the skin to as deep as two inches. Sometimes the needles were left in for only a second, other times for ten to fifteen seconds; sometimes they were turned very rapidly, other times not at all.

Dr. Siow began at my right wrist. The first needle was inserted and turned. I felt a mild sensation bordering on discomfort. Then, in rapid succession, insertions were made in the forearm and the elbow. He repeated similar insertions along my left arm. A few times I felt the prick of the needle, but no more pain than that. The needle was placed in several points on the lower part of my forehead, perhaps a half-inch above the eyes. Again, no pain; rather it felt as if my protoplasm was being rearranged. Then there were several insertions on each side of the neck where it joins the head. The needle was turned rapidly and it felt like a screw was turning, churning away at the cells. But it was not painful.

Dr. Siow then had me lie down on the treatment table. First I lay on my back and rapid pricks were made on my stomach, knees, ankles, and the tops of my feet. Then I turned over and needles were placed in several places along my spinal cord, in the kidney area, and in the backs of my knees. Some of the needles in the stomach and back were mildly painful, but only for a split second.

Dr. Fischer recorded his impressions of the first treatment as follows: "These began with Mr. Tate sitting in a chair. Dr. Siow took out two of his acupuncture needles and gave one of them to me. The needles were made of stainless steel and were about the thickness of a fine wire. This would be finer than our usual 28-gauge injection needles. In fact, they had a certain flexibility to them. They come in various lengths, ranging from about a half-centimeter to three centimeters. Dr. Siow told us later that the needles were generally made of stainless steel and that in earlier times they had been made of iron, rusting easily and requiring considerably more care. He said that he doubted that silver and gold wires had been used in the past, as we had read, because he felt they would not have been strong enough.

"Dr. Siow began by placing needles into the body near the wrists, near the elbows and shoulders. He then placed a needle into the skin of the nose in the midline and then placed them in several places in the neck and upper back. He then had Mr. Tate lie supine on his examining couch and placed needles into the anterior chest, into the anterior abdominal wall, the knees, bi-line, the shins bi-line and the dorsal area of the feet. He then had Mr. Tate assume the prone position and placed the needles in various positions along the spine generally in the paraspinal portion in the low lumbar and sacral regions particularly. Needles were also placed along the iliac crest. The needle was placed in various depths but often penetrated up to two or three centimeters. Dr. Siow placed the needles quite quickly and seemingly with confidence. Occasionally a needle was repositioned slightly. The needles were left in for varying periods of time, some simply for seconds, others for thirty seconds and on one occasion on a later day for approximately ten minutes. Occasionally, with the needle in place, he manipulated the needle, either with a short vibratory motion or with a rotation motion. There seemed to be more care to applying the needles in the wrist area bilaterally. During this first session, Mr. Tate at no time complained of any pain or discomfort associated with the placing of the needles. The needles were stored in a pincushion type of arrangement submerged in alcohol and they were wiped off with an alcohol sponge between each application. Several different needles were used during the course of the entire treatment. The skin was generally very briefly prepared with alcohol before the pins were placed.

"One's overall impression of Dr. Siow was that he was extremely friendly and pleasant. He showed not the slightest resentment or feeling of insecurity that a physician should have accompanied Mr. Tate or asked him questions about his technique. He seemed to have complete confidence in the technique and in every way handled himself in a manner that would have done credit to any physician. In general, he gave the impression of great competence and confidence."

After My First Acupuncture Treatment, I Felt Incredibly Energized

When I was told the treatment was over, I was quite pleased it had gone so well. I stood up and felt remarkably buoyant. My whole body tingled and seemed energized. I remarked on how I felt and Dr. Siow smiled. "And you will feel more relaxed," he said. "You will sleep well tonight." Although I had not slept well since arriving in London, I remained alert and full of energy throughout the rest of the day. Dr. Fischer retired after a late supper and I went out to explore Piccadilly into early morning.

On Tuesday I had my second treatment. After feeling my pulses, Dr. Siow began with the right wrist, then the elbow, then went to my left arm. The needles that felt like screws turning were inserted into my neck. Up to this point, there had been no pain, only mild discomfort. I was therefore surprised when some of the needles he placed in my back along the spinal cord produced severe pain, though of short duration. The pain was deeper and more acute than just being stuck with a pin. Several of the needles caused a strange kind of burning pain. As bad as the sensations were, however, they did not compare with the pain caused by one needle placed in the leg under my left knee. It felt as though I had been electrocuted from my knee to my toes and that my leg consisted of a thousand fibers which had suffered a terrible shock. After I recovered from the sensation, I made a mental note that it could be described only as extremely, extremely painful. The pain caused by several needles in the stomach was also acute. One needle over the liver sent pain through my right side. I was concerned that this needle might have entered my liver and asked Dr. Fischer about it later. He agreed that the insertion was rather deep and could have pierced the liver but said that the needles are so fine, no damage could be done. I still remember quite clearly a needle Dr. Siow inserted near my navel which caused pain to shoot down into the groin.

Each time I felt pain, I did not try to hide it. I could not do otherwise but wince and sometimes yelp, because, quite simply, it hurt like hell. Dr. Siow was unperturbed. When I asked him about the pain later on, he said it was a good sign because it showed that my nerves were becoming energized and alive.

I told Dr. Siow that the articles I had read indicated acupuncture was at worst uncomfortable, but not very painful. He responded that the type of acupuncture practiced by most Western physicians did not cause pain because the needles pierced only the skin and did not touch the nerves. That type of treatment was usually ineffective or at best caused only temporary cures.

After four treatments, Dr. Siow told me that he wanted to see me again in a month. I quickly agreed to return to London in late June, for I was convinced that Dr. Siow was a master healer. I had spoken with many of his patients. I had discussed acupuncture theory with Dr. Siow at length, and he had allowed me to read a file of articles that he had written or had been written about him. I was extremely impressed.

Dr. Siow, By Western Standards, Performs Miracles

The patients in the waiting room freely discussed their ailments and why they had come to Dr. Siow. Many of their friends had been cured of illnesses such as arthritis, migraine, chronic back pain, gout, and a host of other diseases. I met a young man from Holland whose sight and speech had been restored by Dr. Siow. Dr. Siow was still working to restore the man's hearing. I spoke with another man, also from Holland, who had suffered a spinal cord injury as the result of a disk problem and had been paralyzed from the waist down. His doctors had told him to get used to a wheelchair because he would never walk again. The man refused to listen. He heard about Dr. Siow and begged him to come to Holland to make a diagnosis. Dr. Siow went to the man's home where he lay bedridden and began treatment immediately. There was some response in his legs, and the man moved to London so that he could have intensive treatment for several months. When I saw him, he was walking on crutches and was able to drive a car. He was hoping for further improvement.

One of the articles I read about Dr. Siow said the doctor claimed to have cured cancer on the hands, arms, legs, and necks of many people in Britain. He was quoted as saying that a cure for cancer of the organs could be found because all cancer, he believed, was related to the "nerves." Years later, he reported he cured cancer of the liver when found in an early stage. I asked Dr. Siow about treating cancer with acupuncture and he said that he could cure cancer in 60 percent of all cases unless the cancer was in an advanced stage where it affected the organs.

In June, Judy and I went back to Spain with Chris and Dave, who were then five and three, to visit friends we had met in 1968. En route we stopped in London to see Dr. Siow. He treated me only twice. After the second treatment he said that my pulses showed that I was now in balance. He had been able to tone up the liver and now the imbalance was gone.

To maintain general good health, he suggested that I walk quickly "like a soldier walks" for about a half hour each morning and a half hour each evening. He also recommended a drink of brandy before retiring.

During the summer following the treatment, there was a marked change in my body. My energy level greatly increased. I noticed that when I played tennis or worked outside, I would sweat much more profusely than I ever had before. My appetite increased and I began to crave more starches and vegetables and less meat. Within three months I gained 14 pounds, going from 144 to 158.

Dr. Siow had told me that I was "in balance." When I asked him if I should come back in six months or a year, he replied that it would not be necessary. Nevertheless, I continue to make an annual visit to his tiny office on Preston Road in Wembley. For as the proverb says, "The superior doctor prevents illness." And Dr. Siow is a superior doctor.

CHAPTER 10

Means of Survival: Psychic Healing

When I was in London in 1972 for acupuncture treatments, I visited a bookstore near Leicester Square. One of the books I arbitrarily pulled from the shelf was *The Nature of Healing* by Arthur Guirdham. Dr. Guirdham was a British psychiatrist who lived outside of Bath. He had practiced psychiatry for over forty years and had written numerous books on healing and other topics. His books had been translated into the world's major languages.

After reading *The Nature of Healing*, I seriously considered for the first time whether psychic healing might have any validity. Various writers distinguish among "psychic healing," "faith healing," "natural healing," and "spiritual healing," but I tend to place them in the same category. For me, psychic healing is the transmittal of "energy," which some call God, prana, life-force, Christ-consciousness, et cetera, from or through one person for the purpose of healing, or accelerating self-healing in the latter.

Dr. Guirdham wrote his book to demonstrate that there are innate gifts of healing that function independently of the science and art of medicine. He believed that man was in the process of evolving into a new and psychic dimension and the book was to be his "widow's mite" contribution to the "surge of anti-materialism which at this moment is erupting from the universal mind into the consciousness of man."

Trained as a scientist, Dr. Guirdham had no particular interest in natural healing. Then evidence for its existence was thrust upon him. When he could no longer ignore it, he decided to investigate the phenomenon of people apparently curing disease without recourse to medicine.

I found Dr. Guirdham's narrative both fascinating and convincing. His honesty of observation and reporting was apparent. More important, the theoretical basis he posited for natural healing seemed eminently reasonable. The authority with which he spoke assured me that what he was saying was probably true.

To understand his theory, we must begin with his ideas about personality. He tells us we have two selves: personality, which is the weapon we construct for ourselves with which we face the hazards of life in the community, and what he calls "The You which is not You." The latter is our real and transcendental self through which we are able to maintain contact with the universal consciousness that permeates all things.

What is meant by universal consciousness? We are all part of a common, universal, and timeless mind. Behind the curtain of our personalities, we are each of us in contact with the infinite. Occasionally, due to no efforts of our own, there is a gap in the curtain. We see the continuity of all things and the unity of creation. Sometimes this gap in the curtain admits enough light for someone to be healed by it. The universal consciousness exists outside the confines of our personality. It is the ultimate essence from which we all are derived. It surrounds us everywhere and permeates us invisibly and inaudibly. Occasionally it speaks to us or reveals itself to us more clearly. For the most part, we shut ourselves off from it.

When Healing Occurs, the Healer and the Healed Have, for the Moment, a Common Soul

The person who is a healer is able to open herself to the universal consciousness. When this happens, the two individuals, the healer and the healed, have, for the moment, a common soul. This fusion of two souls that occurs in healing is really a returning to the universal consciousness in which disease is impossible. It is a matter that transcends the healer and the healed. It is a re-entering, on part of both, into the common consciousness of the universe.

One of the chapters in Dr. Guirdham's book is entitled "Cure by Revelation." In it he describes cases in which patients who, for no "valid" reason and because of no special treatment, state with the force of religious conviction that they are immeasurably better and that they know they will not relapse. When I completed his book, I wrote to Dr. Guirdham to tell him of my own "revelation"—the day in my study when I declared myself cured. I also wanted to thank him for the enlightenment that he gave me. In a short time, I received a reply. Among other things, he wrote, "It seems that your experience has followed pretty well on the same lines as my own, that is to say, you had certain potentialities and these were overlaid by education and what have you. I suffered from an overdose of 'science.' It seems to me that reawakening is often associated with disease. I have seen this in my own case. At times it is difficult to know if the disease is cause or effect. Sometimes it carries a message. Sometimes it is the result of a message resisted. In any case I am very pleased that all is going well with you."

Some years later, while on another trip to London for acupuncture, I had the weekend free and decided to take a train into the English countryside. For no apparent reason, I decided to visit Bath. I then remembered that Dr. Guirdham lived there but felt awkward about calling him on such short notice. Nevertheless, when I arrived late on Saturday afternoon, I telephoned him. I told him who I was and asked if it would be possible to see him on Sunday. I assured him that if he was busy, I would certainly understand.

"Well," he said in his marvelous British way, "let me have a look at my schedule. I was just going out the door. . . ."

After a pause, he said, "I hope you don't think me a dog, but I'll only be able to see you for an hour tomorrow. You see, we have an engagement at noon. Why don't you come at about eleven?"

That night, while meditating, I tried to visualize what Dr. Guirdham looked like. I "saw" a tall, portly man with thinning white hair and a full patrician face.

Dr. Guirdham's home was in the countryside outside of Bath. In the midst of gentle, rolling hills and farmland, the region is soothing to the eyes and the spirit. Mrs. Guirdham, a gracious lady, met me at the door and introduced me to her husband. I could not help but remark, "Yes, you're exactly as I visualized you last night."

Mrs. Guirdham served tea and then we all sat down for what was for me an exciting, often exhilarating hour. My impression was that Dr. Guirdham was an intellectual giant. I felt I was in the presence of a Freud or Jung. We (for the most part, he) covered many topics: reincarnation, religion, healing, acupuncture, out-of-body experiences, etiology of disease, the misuse of drugs. He decried the use of drugs for instant enlightenment and criticized those who advocated such use. As for the causation of disease, he believed that illness, generally speaking, has several concomitant causes. In order for a person to get cancer, he might, for example, have a genetic predisposition, be exposed to a carcinogen, and be psychologically and emotionally "receptive" to the disease. Dr. Guirdham also believed that there is a cultural factor to disease. Thus people in certain areas of the world seem prone to diseases almost indigenous to the region, and the relationship cannot be explained by hygienic practices.

About noon Dr. Guirdham offered to drive me back to Bath. He gave me a quick tour of the city, pointing out the houses where many famous English writers had once lived. It seemed he knew the poets' works by heart, for more than once, when mentioning a name, he would recite a poem or two. It did not seem he was reciting the poetry for my benefit but rather was conjuring the poet's presence, allowing him to live again through his words.

My visit with Dr. Guirdham convinced me that psychic healing was real. I did not feel the need, however, to experience it. Then, in the autumn of 1974, I attended a parapsychology conference. One of the many interesting speakers was a woman by the name of Olga Worrall. Mrs. Worrall looked like the grandmother next door. In her late sixties, she had graying hair and a kindly face. She told us matter-of-factly that she was a healer and has been healing people for over fifty years. She had discovered her gift as a child. Her touch or presence had been able to make her sick mother well. She was soon asked to exert the same influence on sick neighbors.

Mrs. Worrall thought of herself as a mutant, although to her, her healing abilities were very natural. Like most healers she did not claim to be the source of healing power, but only its instrument. "God does the healing," she was quick to say.

Olga Worrall's Presence Inspired a Strange Elation

When I was in Mrs. Worrall's presence that afternoon, I felt strangely elated, and I knew that the source of this physical and mental well-being was Mrs. Worrall. I decided then that I would visit the church in Baltimore where every Thursday morning she participated in a healing service. In her lecture she had spoken of spiritual healing as similar to charging someone's batteries. Disease, she stressed, was unnatural, and the body in most instances can cure itself. Once in a while, the body is overwhelmed by a disease and the person needs help. This help may be medical, spiritual, or both. Spiritual help involves the transfer of energy akin to "charging the sick person's batteries." With the extra boost, the sick person's self-healing mechanism is once again able to function. I didn't think I needed the extra boost to remain well, as I felt I was already whole, but I could not let this opportunity pass.

A few months later I went to Baltimore. I arrived at the Mount Washington Methodist Church shortly before ten on a Thursday morning. The lower church, a large structure made of stone, was built in 1860. The service was held in the upper church, which had been built over the older stone building.

Mrs. Worrall appeared shortly after ten. She was dressed in a black robe but looked cheerful in her turquoise necklace and earrings. After welcoming everyone, she gave a brief lecture on auras—the phenomenon of the body emitting an energy field that some people are able to see. She told us that her deceased husband, Ambrose, also a healer, had said that every part of the body gives off an aura. An aura registers a person's state of health as well as his spiritual development.

Mrs. Worrall also spoke of negative thoughts which can have an adverse affect on people who are receptive to them. "We are One," she said. "We can affect each other with our goodness and badness."

After the talk, the service began. Two Methodist ministers and a Catholic priest led us in prayers and hymns. One of the ministers gave an excellent sermon on healing. We were told the search for healing and wholeness must begin with ourselves. Disharmony does not come from God or the divine. Illness is a disruption of natural law. If we violate laws, we do so at risk. We determine our own circumstances and not vice versa. A cure is a response to our own cooperation with love, medicine, and God. We must open our lives to the wholesome influence of God and friends. Spiritual healing occurs when we rid ourselves of reservations and accept all that is offered to us in the divine presence.

After the sermon (there was no collection and offerings are not accepted), Mrs. Worrall announced that the healing service would begin. The two ministers, the priest, and Mrs. Worrall came forward to the rail that was in the front of the church. She asked that the children be brought up first. Two men came from the back carrying a little girl of about four. She was severely deformed. She was blind in one eye, which was all scar tissue, and she wore special shoes and braces. Mrs. Worrall asked that she be brought to the first pew. There, she very tenderly put her hands around the girl's head. She then embraced the little girl, held her in her arms for three or four minutes. Then a little black boy of about three who had cerebral palsy was carried to Mrs. Worrall. She held him very closely for several minutes.

Meanwhile some adults were walking up to the three men and receiving the laying on of hands. They would kneel down before the healer and the healer would place his hands on the person's head or the back of the neck and sometimes the back. The healer would usually close his eyes and remain in this position for about a minute. After several minutes, I walked to the line of people in front of Mrs. Worrall. When my turn came, I stood in front of her and, in response to her questions, told her what my problem had been. I told her I felt assured I was now cured.

She said, "I want you to stand and I want to put my hands around your pancreas." She then placed one hand over my solar plexus and one on my back. "Don't be so tense. Relax. You're too tight."

When Mrs. Worrall Touched Me, I Felt Warm, Vibratory Energy Moving Up My Spine

I tried to relax, to put everything out of my mind. Then I felt some kind of vibration coming from her hands. A strange, vibratory energy traveled up my spine. Then I felt a warmth emanating from her hands which was soothing. Her hands were on me for about a minute. As she removed her hands, Mrs. Worrall told me to take a drink of unsweetened grape juice every day. I returned to my seat awestruck. The sensations I had experienced were strong and pronounced. I hadn't imagined them. How strange, I thought. How very strange. Believing that someone could transmit energy through her hands was one thing. Experiencing it was quite another. I couldn't wait to tell Judy what had happened.

After the service, I joined fifty or so other people for a luncheon downstairs. I sat across from Mrs. Worrall and felt the same uplifting power I had experienced the afternoon I first heard her speak. I watched her interact with people and was impressed by her great warmth. She reminded me to take the grape juice every day, a large glass around lunchtime. I have, of course, followed her advice, and I now prefer the drink above all others.

I should mention that I did not witness any dramatic cures either during or after the service. While dramatic cures have occurred during a healing service, Mrs. Worrall told me they are rare. When psychic healing does take place, it is usually a gradual process.

I had a number of questions I wanted to ask Mrs. Worrall. I had even brought a tape recorder so that I could bring home her voice and words. She graciously agreed to answer my questions. I first asked her about the causes of disease. Why do people become ill?

"We should make every effort not to run down our bodies and not abuse them through drink, et cetera. We have a tremendous responsibility to take care of our bodies and if we don't we are going to pay the price. That's the law. Now in many cases illness is brought about because of ignorance of the laws. People do not observe the laws of sanitation, do not observe the laws of good eating. Unfortunately, our young women are not taught how to cook properly. They don't know the first thing about diet. They know all about sex but they don't know the first thing about food. There are many, many factors which cause illness, but one of the things we must avoid is to give people guilt feelings to make them feel that they did a terrible thing, that they're sinners and God won't heal them. In the case of babies that are malformed at birth, in many cases it is the result of the ignorance of the doctors. A woman will be given drugs while she's pregnant. No woman should take a drug while she's pregnant, because it will affect the baby. Or a child might be injured during the delivery when forceps are used or the delivery has been rushed. And then of course we must remember that some of the malformations are genetic. I feel that we are very, very particular how we breed animals, but we are not particular how we breed humans. If there is a genetic illness, these people should not procreate."

Spiritual Healing Should Be an Adjunct to Traditional Medical Care

"It behooves all of us to try to do as good a job at keeping as well as possible. Then, if we are the unfortunate victims of ill health, we should make every effort to correct it. How? By making sure we go to the root of the problem. Now if it's genetic, our hands are tied. But we can better it, with the proper approach, the attitude of mind, using the various approaches of medicine. I am a firm believer in osteopathic medicine. A lot of the damage that is done to a baby can be immediately corrected to prevent in later years problems of a mal-formed back or something of that sort. I feel that we should use all the arts of healing, including prayer, the right attitude of mind—constructive thinking is so important, you know. We should use proper medical attention and should apply spiritual healing as an adjunct. We are not replacing the medical doctor or medical talents. We are adding that extra ingredient and I feel that a person who is thus blessed, shall we say designated by God to be a carrier for His energy, triggers off or accelerates the normal healing processes of the physical body, gives the body that added boost and then the body can get well."

Q: "Do you think that healing is a continuous process?"

A: "You're constantly healing. Your body is constantly being replaced. You're not the same as you were a few minutes ago. We're all born with a built-in healing mechanism. And this takes care of our bodies during our lifetime, but if we abuse our body or if our body has a traumatic experience, the battery runs down. So what do you do? The same as with a car battery: You boost it. So spiritual healing is a battery charger. And it accelerates the healing process, gives it that extra boost so that the person can regain control over his body."

Q: "In terms of the source, I know that you say that God—"

A: "That's right. There's only one source, the creator of all creation. Some call it God. Some call it Law. Some say it is the Supreme Intelligence. I don't care what you call it, it is the same."

Q: "I know you are familiar with the work of Lawrence LeShan."

A: "I know him, Larry, very well. We knew him before he went into that work."

Q: "He seems to take the God factor out of it and seems to say that—"

A: "I don't think that Larry takes the God factor out. Remember that he is not a Christian and we Christians are too prone to use that word God, Jesus, something. A non-Christian is not apt to use that term. It doesn't matter. It doesn't matter what you call it so long as it works. Whether you call it God or the energy or whatever you want to call it, it's still the same source."

Q: "In one, you pray. You wouldn't pray to an energy source, or would you? Do you pray while you heal?"

A: "I am constantly aware of the presence of this energy, this presence, this power, call it what you will. I do not pray like the average person would be praying. I don't lament to God, I don't beseech God. I know it's there and God wants me to use it. God, intelligence, divine power, whatever name you want to call it, it is there waiting to be used. I focus that energy onto the person who comes to me for help. And so I am a channel. I am so biologically constructed that this energy can flow through me. And I probably act as a transformer transforming it into an energy that can be utilized by the individual. It's so simple and we mustn't complicate it by words. Words can really lead us astray. We have to just let the power flow.

"I have been healing in the Methodist church for twenty-five years and, as you know, we don't take any money at all. We are sharing our gift and therefore are not a threat to established medicine because we are not stealing their thunder or their business. Now let me add this. If a person is giving his entire time to it, he should be paid for his time. The gift is free. But if he has no other means of income, he should be paid for his time."

Q: "You don't devote your full time to the healing ministry?"

A: "Let me say that I devote about seventy-five percent of my time, but fortunately my husband and I decided that we were not going to take money for our healing gifts. We wanted this to be our avocation and my husband was an executive with a well-known company and he footed the bill for our expenses."

Healers Should Have a Place in Houses of Worship

"I feel that there should be a healer in every church and every synagogue. We have a lot of Jewish people here today because they can't go to their own temple or synagogue to get it. The Jewish people knew about spiritual healing. Look at Moses and the prophets who healed their people. So this is very biblical. One woman came to me today and said, 'I feel like I'm an interloper because I am of the Jewish faith.' I said, 'You're still my sister.' I feel this way. If each church would provide a healing service for its people, it would be working with the medical profession and people. People would be getting well. Peace of mind is so important."

Q: "What about people's attitudes toward disease?"

A: "We teach them that they have got to get well fast and not concentrate on the disease or illness. Emphasize the positive. Change your thinking."

The Lawrence LeShan I referred to in the interview is a clinical psychologist who is also a healer. Dr. LeShan was not a "born" healer, i.e., he did not manifest any healing abilities before he began to study the phenomenon of psychic healing. After years of study and practice, he was able to achieve a state of consciousness in which he was able to heal. He describes his adventure, a "search for the meaning of impossible events," in his book *The Medium, the Mystic and the Physicist.*

Dr. LeShan's work raises the fascinating question of whether healers can be trained. Dr. Guirdham believes that healers are "born," not "made," and Mrs. Worrall's views appear to be similar. But others, including Dr. LeShan, believe that psychic healing is a faculty that is latent in all of us and that through rigorous meditative exercises and the desire and compassion to love in this manner, this latent ability can be freely exercised. For years Dr. LeShan conducted training workshops in New York City for people who wished to develop their healing abilities, and from what I have read, the trainees are sometimes able to effect positive change in the health of others.

In order to learn more about developing healing ability, I attended a two-day workshop. The workshop was conducted by Bruce Gregory, who studied with Dr. LeShan and who was a Silva Mind Control instructor.

Like the mind control course, Bruce's workshop had two aspects: content and conditioning cycles, or meditation exercises. He began by telling us health and happiness are normal and disease may be looked upon as the inhibition of the "soul" or spiritual life of a person. It may begin as a psychosomatic response caused by stress or the frustration of creative desires. When disease does strike, we should strive to learn the lesson it brings. When sick, we should try to love more. Recovery comes most quickly when we have a good reason for living. We should love our bodies and show this love through proper diet and exercise. Our minds should always be positive, and we should be aware that we "create" our own emotional state.

Healing should be done without a sense of attachment. The "ego" should be kept out of the act. As healers, we are releasing the Real, not recreating it. There are many ways of healing, but all healing seems to require a subtle cooperation between the healer, the healed person, and God. No one part of the system can be healed without the other. There must be a balance in body, mind, emotions, and spirit.

Most of the people at the workshop were familiar with meditation. Bruce tried to have us go deeper in meditation through various breathing and visualization techniques. While in these states, we practiced healing one another by the laying on of hands. Most of us did not feel or experience anything unusual. Many, however, did feel a transfer of heat or energy. My brother attempted to cure a woman of deafness in one ear. While doing so, he felt a tremendous force of energy coming from his hands. The woman felt nothing and her hearing did not improve. A few minutes later he directed this energy to his own ankle, which he had sprained and which was causing him discomfort. The pain disappeared immediately and his ankle never bothered him again.

Not long after the workshop I went back to see Mrs. Worrall, this time with my brother. When Mrs. Worrall shook his hands, she remarked, "Oh, you're a healer." She explained she could feel the healing energy in his hands. Frank—like Mrs. Worrall, as I think of it—is down-to-earth. A lawyer and certified public accountant, he was a judge at the time. He took Mrs. Worrall's comments in stride. But in the months that followed I heard stories from common friends that he was curing people of headaches.

A few years later he developed and began teaching a course in meditation and self-healing techniques. More than once I was there when someone complained of a headache. Frank would walk over to him or her, as if it were a perfectly natural thing to do, and would place his hands on the person's head while he closed his eyes. Within a minute or two, the person reported the headache was gone, and

Frank would return to his lecture as if nothing significant had happened.

Recently I experienced some discomfort in my lower abdomen and back. The discomfort quickly escalated to excruciating pain. I was barely able to drive to the emergency room. When I got there, the triage nurse said my condition—it turned out to be a kidney stone—did not appear life-threatening. I would have a long wait—they were very busy. I called my brother and then lay on a cot in the corridor moaning and cursing. When Frank arrived, he placed his hands on my stomach and back. The pain immediately receded. I could still feel it, but I was detached from it. It was easy to bear. I had to wait over an hour before I saw a physician. My brother's hands were the only analgesic I needed.

CHAPTER 11

Means of Survival: Inspirational Literature

T he year following my chemotherapy passed quickly. And then another. During that time I went to see Dr. Fischer in New Haven every three months. I also went to Albany Medical Center for checkups in the oncology clinic. I always hated those visits. As soon as I walked in the clinic door, I no longer felt like a person but like a patient. I experienced the old rage as I waited for the nurse to call my name. The physical examination by one of the clinic doctors was always quick. I was told that I "seemed to be doing well." That was as optimistic as they allowed themselves to be. After two years they told me to report every six months. Checkup time always came too quickly.

In contrast, the trips to New Haven were not unpleasant. It is true that I wasted little time in leaving the city once my examination with Dr. Fischer was over. The memories that the city produced were harsh. But I was greeted by Dr. Fischer more as a friend than as a patient. We spent as long as half an hour chatting about everything from the weather to the latest developments in radiation therapy. At some point the conversation ended and the examination, always extremely thorough, began. But the transition was natural.

The Conviction That You're in Perfect Health Should Come From Within

Dr. Fischer's statements—"everything's fine"—always brought relief. I tried, however, not to need or depend on medical opinion for proof that I was well. The proof of my state of perfect health had to come from within.

I began the process of healing with an idea—the idea that I was cured. It was the idea that I had to rely on. The idea had to sustain me.

I spent a great deal of time thinking about the power of ideas. I had come to believe that the "stuff" of the material world is an expression of the idea-forms of mind. As I think of my body, so it becomes.

I had even worked out the beginnings of a theory, not original, but one that was "mine" nonetheless: Ideas are a function of mind; they are generated by mind. But mind is not really a distinct entity. It is such an intimate part of the mind-body complex that the material aspect—the body—is often the sole or at least a concomitant catalyst for thought.

A simple example. We experience a pain in the head. We think, "I have a headache." An experience in the body has given rise to a thought. The situation can be made a bit more complex if we add a thought component to the equation. "I have a headache (body-induced thought) because I'm under pressure to complete an assignment (mind-induced thought)." The underlying premise, which may or may not be verbalized in the conscious mind, is: Whenever I'm under pressure, I get a headache. This premise is perhaps a realistic inference based upon repeated experience. But when the mind accepts it as Idea, it acquires power. The mind informs the body, Whenever I'm under pressure to complete an assignment, I get a headache. The body is "formed" by both the thought and the expectation of its realization.

In order for the pattern or association between "pressure" and "headache" to be broken, two things must occur. The negative thought or "program" must be discontinued, and a positive "program" must be inserted in its place: "I will feel healthy and good throughout my body, especially my head, at all times. I can handle pressure well, and I will feel particularly good before, during, and after working on tough assignments."

I Choose to Believe—I Must Believe—That the Mind Can Help Heal the Body

The example I have described is an expression of my belief system, which was derived from what I have learned and have chosen to accept as true. I will be the first to admit that I have chosen this belief system because I have a vested interest in its validity. I not only believe that the mind controls, informs, and thus can make the body whole; I *have* to believe these things. For it may well be that I remain healthy and alive solely because of my belief. I think again of the tightrope hundreds of feet above the ground. I realize that I have created the rope in my mind. No matter. If I doubt its reality, it will disappear. No matter. I believe in the rope. The rope is *real.* The rope supports me.

In *Tales of Power,* Carlos Casteneda discusses *having to believe.* Don Juan, a Yaqui Indian shaman, tells him, "In other words, the secret of a warrior is that he believes without believing. But obviously a warrior cannot just say he believes and let it go at that. That would be too easy. To just believe would exonerate him from examining his situation. A warrior, whenever he has to involve himself with believing, does it as a choice, an expression of innermost predilection. A warrior doesn't believe, a warrior has to believe. . . . death is the indispensable ingredient in having to believe."

I believe because I must believe. The image of being suspended hundreds of feet in the air with only the rope keeping me from falling to my death is awesome. But belief in the rope is not so difficult when I realize that many other people believe in similar ropes.

That is the value of what I term "inspirational literature." Inspirational literature is any writing which reinforces my belief that my mind has the power to heal my body and to keep it perfectly healthy.

I have been and continue to be inspired by Casteneda's works, by the Seth books, by *Jonathan Livingston Seagull,* and by many of the articles in *Unity Magazine,* to name a few.

Rather than attempt a synthesis of the many ideas found in these writings, which would be a near-impossible task, I will discuss a few passages from some of the books.

From *Seth Speaks* by Jane Roberts:

> You usually do not realize that your physical body is created by you each moment as a direct result of your inner conception of what you are, or that it changes in important chemical and electromagnetic ways with the ever-moving pace of your own thought.
>
> This may seem strange, but all acts are mental, or if you would prefer, psychic acts. This is an extremely simple explanation; but the thought creates the reality. Illness is often the result of ignorance and lazy mental habits.
>
> We go back to our fundamentals: you create reality through your feelings, thoughts and mental actions. Some of these are physically materialized, others are actualized in probable systems. You are presented with an endless series of choices, it seems, at any point, some more or less favorable than others. You must understand that each mental act is a reality for which you are responsible.

The above passages affirm the power of the mind to create or alter the physical body. A somewhat more mystical and more subtle expression of a similar idea is found in *A Separate Reality,* another Casteneda book. Don Juan has said that one of the tools of a warrior is "will." He then tries to explain what he means by the term.

"Will is something very special. It happens mysteriously. There is no real way of telling how one uses it, except that the results of using the will are astonishing. Perhaps the first thing that one should do is to know that one can develop will."

Casteneda asks, "What exactly is the will? Is it determination, like the determination of your grandson Lucio to have a motorcycle?"

> "No," Don Juan said softly and giggled. "That's not will. Lucio only indulges. Will is something else, something clear and powerful which can direct our acts. *Will is something man uses, for instance, to win a battle which he, by all calculations, should lose."* [Emphasis mine.]
>
> "Then will must be what we call courage," I said.

"No. Courage is something else. Men of courage are dependable men, noble men perennially surrounded by people who flock around them and fearless men who are given to performing daring common-sense acts; most of the time a courageous man is also fearsome and feared. Will, on the other hand, has to do with astounding feats that defy our common sense."

I have applied the truth of Don Juan's statements in a variety of contexts. Its application in the area of health is obvious.

More direct statements about healing are contained in a remarkable little booklet called "The Unity Guide to Healing," which I obtained free by writing *Unity*, Unity Village, Missouri 64065. This booklet is filled with chunks of inspirational wisdom:

> Health is the natural state of man. The word *to heal* comes from the Saxon *helian:* to cover, to conceal, to be made whole. Thus a healthy man is a whole one, one who lives and functions just as his Creator intended him to. Health is fundamental in Being and health is man's divine birthright. It is the orderly state of existence, and man must learn to use the knowledge of this truth to sustain the consciousness of health.

After rereading such broadly worded passages several times, I try to reduce them to concrete concepts which my mind can readily grasp. Thus, I tell myself, "I am whole," and I let this thought fill my body. I try to have my body feel the message. "I am whole; I am clean; I am pure; I am, and will continue to be, in a state of perfect health."

Another statement from the Unity Guide reinforced what I had discovered about attitude:

> Our free and happy feeling about ourself abets the healing flow, whereas our anxiety concerning our state of health can disturb and distress the natural working of the body.

Of all the attitudes necessary for health, probably the most difficult to sustain is a "happy feeling about ourself." It is a feeling of "safe-ness," of internal warmth and security—the feeling that everything is all right. When we have been seriously ill, it is far easier to worry and to be anxious about our bodies. It is particularly difficult to feel confident that our bodies are healing when we experience symptoms, real or imagined.

> Only one healing power exists, whether evoked by methods of physician, witch doctor, or metaphysician. The goal is not surgery for its own sake, or medication for its own sake, or even prayer for its own sake. These methods are employed to release the inherent healing power and to restore the body to its normal condition of health. Whether the life principle's energy is activated by meditation or by medication makes no difference.

I have found this theme repeated again and again in the "inspirational literature." Ultimately, the body heals itself. This is true even of cancer. For some time it was the prevalent belief among physicians (and perhaps still is) that in order to cure a cancer patient, you must "get it all"—all cancerous cells in the body must be destroyed. If they aren't, then the cells left behind will multiply and overcome the body's defenses once again.

I don't believe that's true. The task of the physician, through the mechanical means available to him or to her, is to remove or kill as many of the diseased cells as possible so that the body's natural defenses will be able to kill or render harmless the rest. Dr. Fischer once told me that he no longer believes that total kill is necessary for cure. And my friend Robert, who became an oncologist, said that some patients continue to have cellular evidence of cancer but remain otherwise healthy and free of symptoms.

I do believe it's important, perhaps crucial, that the body's natural defenses be triggered. I believe this can be accomplished by "speaking to the body" in meditation, using methods like those taught at Silva Mind Control. The defenses can also be activated when "energy" is transferred from or through a psychic healer. But what of people, I ask myself, who do not know that the body must heal itself? The chances are they will never be told by their physicians. I suspect that in most cases the trauma of illness automatically activates the body's healing mechanism. But I firmly believe we should use every tool at our disposal, particularly our minds, to enhance this process.

People Shouldn't Blame Themselves for Getting Sick Or Not Recovering Their Health

What about those writers, many of whom have inspired me, who suggest that a sick person is to blame for his or her illness? This is a difficult issue, one that is not always handled well. I certainly don't want to contribute to the wrongness of the blame philosophy. I wrote earlier that in some sense I felt responsible for bringing about my illness. This was my experience, my truth, but I would never extend it beyond myself. Although I might have been responsible, I don't blame myself. When I dropped out of graduate school and entertained those suicidal images, I did not realize that I might be harming myself. If someone had told me then, "Don't do that; it might be dangerous," I would have stopped. I did not knowingly or willingly harm myself. And so I don't blame myself for what occurred.

I think of those who try to cure themselves by every possible means and still don't recover their health. Should they be made to feel guilty? Or think of themselves as failures? I don't think so. Not at all. I think the proper attitude is one expressed by Norman Cousins: *Give it your best shot.* That's all anyone, including yourself, can expect.

My testimony is not about the acceptance of death. Many people have written eloquently on that subject. The thrust of my message is about healing and survival. That has been my path and my struggle. Many people whose opinions I respect would disagree with my approach, calling it one-sided. My response is that I am not writing a philosophy of life—what one ought to think or do—but bearing witness to my own experience and the ideas which were formed from that experience.

I don't have answers to a number of difficult questions. One, "Should you ever give up?" is especially troublesome. It was answered, however, by a man who I believe was a saint. He was both a Hindu and a Christian and his writing has had a profound effect on me. I am speaking of Paramahansa Yogananda, who is most famous for his extraordinary story, *Autobiography of a Yogi.* I quote from his tiny gem of a book entitled *Scientific Healing Affirmations:*

Attention and Faith are Necessary

All affirmations, in order to reach the superconsciousness, must be free from uncertainties and doubts. Attention and faith are lights that lead even imperfectly understood affirmations to the subconscious and superconscious minds.

Patience and attentive, intelligent repetition are wonder-workers. Affirmations for curing chronic mental or bodily afflictions should be repeated often, deeply and continuously (utterly ignoring unchanged or contrary conditions, if any), until they become part of one's profound intuitional convictions. It is better to die, if death has to come, with the conviction of perfect health than with the thought that a mental or physical ailment is incurable.

Though death may be the necessary end of the body according to present human knowledge, still its "destined hour" may be changed by the power of the soul.

PART III.

Transformation

CHAPTER 12

My Search for Wholeness

M y search for healing has always been a search for wholeness. The connection between these two concepts was made for me in "The Unity Guide to Healing," quoted in the last chapter. *To heal* comes from the Old Saxon *helian* and means *to be made whole.* I also realized that healing is a continuous process and that my search for wholeness would continue throughout my life.

What does it mean to be whole? Although I cannot satisfactorily answer that question, I do know that wholeness has many dimensions: the physical, the emotional, the psychological or mental, and the spiritual. I think of the first three as being within the realm of personality and the latter as being within the realm of spirit or soul.

I have described many of the things I did on the physical, emotional, and psychological levels to help myself heal. Change on the spiritual dimension required a transformation. By that I mean a change in my nature—who I am—or at the very least a change in who I perceived myself to be.

My transformation was a gradual process (and certainly one that still continues), but as I look back, certain markers, particular events, seemed to accelerate it. Although I did not plan these incidents, I was ready for them when they occurred.

Part of the change that came with wanting to be healed was an openness to any thought, to any person, to any experience that might enlighten me. In searching for healing, for the meaning of health, for the meaning of wholeness, I found not only answers, but also questions that were deeper and more intriguing than the ones I had first asked.

My Loss of Faith Was a Slow Process

The significance of these questions for me can only be understood in the context of my religious beliefs. I was raised a Roman Catholic, attended a Catholic high school and Jesuit colleges. I firmly believed in the teachings of the Church and went to mass regularly. Like many Catholics I was often disturbed by the rigidity of the rules and by the means which the Church used to extract conformance with those rules: the threat of eternal damnation. But I accepted the view that the flaws in the institution were due to the imperfections of the people and did not reflect on the validity of the Church as the instrument Christ chose to carry on His work.

I believed in a personal God, a God to Whom I could talk and pray. Whenever I thought I might be seriously ill, I prayed to this God. I have already recalled going to confession the Saturday before the fateful biopsy and telling the priest about my great fear; and his response, so inadequate, so lacking in compassion. He was angry because I had missed mass. He offered me not one word of solace.

I don't know when I "lost my faith," as it is called by the Church. It happened in degrees. A year after my illness had been diagnosed my belief in God began to erode. "God" was, of course, the Judeo-Christian God, the anthropomorphic Father in heaven. At first I wanted to appease Him. I begged, I prayed. But then the anger, the terrible anger began to take hold. In February 1971 I wrote: "Then, when it became apparent that I wasn't going to be struck down with a quick and mighty blow, the juices of my spleen (just before they removed it) began to boil. I was damn angry that this was happening to me. That I might die at an early age and be torn from my wife and children seemed, seems, such an obscenity that I became enraged. But at whom? At God, of course. If you've lived with Him all your life,

He does not go away that easily. And when it hits you that the suffering that some people go through is unspeakable and it is not an abstract proposition but something very real that happens to real people and that it could happen to you, then what do you say to God?

"You say: God, are you crazy? You're allowing this to happen? No one would do that. No man would. Certainly no God would. Not unless He wanted it that way. Not unless He somehow enjoyed it. So is that it? That God is Evil? Well, who knows?

"So it starts to make sense (not good sense perhaps) that that God up there is warped; that He gets some of His kicks from seeing men in anguish. Why else wouldn't He *do* something?

"But what do you do with an evil God? Pray to Him? He might hear you, see? And if He hears you, He might decide to step on you. But if He doesn't know you're there . . . So you become very quiet. . . . Shhhhh. . . . No, you don't pray; you don't even whisper His name; you stop going to church. . . . Maybe He won't see me. So I hid from Him."

But I continued to fear Him. What if He finds me? Will He finish me off? I did not want this evil God threatening me any longer. So I killed him first with my emotions. I wrote, passionately, like a child: "Somewhere up on a hill lives the deity. The hill is always covered in darkness. And there are trees, or rather shrubs, behind which a deity can hide. But if a man sets out, with determination and defiance, and armed with an ax, he has but a chance to meet the deity. He must go in the night and climb the hill. His feet must dig into the earth to brace himself from the wind coming off the hill. And then when he reaches the shrubs, he must go behind each one until the deity is found. He must challenge the deity to a fair fight. And with the ax, he must slay the deity. Then the wind will still and the man will be able to walk from the hill, bleeding slightly from the scratch-wounds, but free. The man will be free."

And I killed him with my intellect. "But then I became more rational. An evil God didn't make sense, did it? After all, who believed in an evil God? Who wants to believe in an evil God? is a better question. No one.

"So, if there couldn't be a good God, and you didn't want an evil God, you were left with no God."

The old God was dead and I was not uncomfortable about it. Months, years passed in this comfortable silence. And during the period that I disengaged from God, my view of man—myself and all of humankind—changed radically. What is the true nature of a being who can "see" inside people thousands of miles away (as I and other students did doing cases at the Silva Mind Control course)? Who are we that some of us can heal others with their hands and prayers?

Are We Essentially Spiritual Beings?

Are we, I often wondered, essentially spiritual beings? Is our consciousness something that exists only because we have a brain? Or can we exist, that is, do we have the potential to exist, outside of our physical bodies? Some light was shed on these questions when I began to have out-of-body experiences.

It was November 3, 1974. I had awakened about 7 A.M. and went to the bathroom to urinate. I returned to our bed and while lying there I saw a tree before my eyes. It was an extraordinarily vivid image and I thought to myself, "How strange. I'm here in bed so I know it's not a real tree. But yet I'm not dreaming." Suddenly I felt a part of me begin to separate from my body. It—this conscious part—moved only a few inches when I became frightened and it quickly reunited with my physical body. I thought, "I've heard about out-of-body experiences. I must be having one. There's no reason to be afraid." I then relaxed. As soon as I did, the conscious part once again separated from my body, this time with a slight jolt. I floated above my body and watched it and Judy sleeping beside me from a point near the ceiling. Then I floated through the walls and found myself flying slowly about thirty feet above the ground to the town where I was born, about fifteen miles away. I could see that I possessed a body, but it was transparent, ethereal. I knew I was not dreaming. I was awake, conscious, in control of my thoughts. I remember thinking that I might not be able to find my body again, but then remembered that others had had this experience and to my knowledge no one had ever gotten "lost." Suddenly, for no apparent reason, I snapped back into my physical body. The reentry was jarring. It was a physical coupling which I likened to two trains linking up. I tried to relax to see if I would go off again, and I did. Moments later I returned.

All of the subsequent out-of-body experiences I had began while I was asleep. Sometimes I would be dreaming an ordinary dream and my mind would suddenly "shatter" the dream. This occurred when I realized I was dreaming. One example is a dream I had of several friends sitting in a restaurant. As soon as I saw them together, I thought, "How very strange. John and Bill would never be sitting together. They don't even know each other. I must be dreaming." With this thought, the dream "shattered" and I was "flung" out of my body. Another recurrent dream I have is of seeing myself in the mirror without a beard (I've had a beard for over twenty years). When I see myself clean-shaven I know I am dreaming, and then I lift out to begin another out-of-body experience.

Right after my first OOBE I wondered, as I wonder now, Who are we that we can leave our physical bodies and continue to be conscious? Are we merely men and women, the most evolved and complex form of animal, or are we something more? My experience of being conscious in a form independent of my ordinary physical body was further evidence for my evolving belief that we are primarily spiritual beings.

Another related phenomenon I experienced was the lucid dream, which is a dream in which we know we are dreaming and yet are able to continue the dream, often controlling it with our thoughts. In my first lucid dream, I was in a store in the town where I was raised and I was perhaps nine or ten. The details of the scene were very clear, very vivid. Suddenly—I don't know why—I realized I was dreaming, but this time I didn't wake up. I, the dreamer, watched the boy leave the store. He stood on the sidewalk. I then thought, "I think I'll have him go right and walk to the post office." As soon as I thought this, the boy turned right and walked in that direction. I realized that whatever I thought was instantaneously translated into the dream reality, which seemed more substantial than life itself. Lucid dreaming gave me the experience of being able to create "reality" with my thoughts.

My "creations," I soon found out, were not unlimited. I once was dreaming of that most beautiful woman, Sophia Loren, and I became lucid in the dream. She was sitting on the other side of the room. The temptation was too much. I thought of myself sitting next to her and as I thought it, it occurred. Then I thought, I will kiss her. And I did. I don't remember my next thought, but I am sure it included the making of passionate love. Unfortunately, the dream shattered and I was thrown into outer space and traveled without even my ethereal or ghostlike body at what seemed like the speed of light. It was an exhilarating but scary ride, and I took it I was being chastised for my lust.

Who Am I? The Question Was Answered with an Experience

Who am I? It's a simple question that seeks to elicit profound answers. It is one of the basic questions that people who think about life's meaning ask themselves. Who am I? Why am I here? Where am I going?

In my case the who-am-I question was answered experientially long before I had consciously asked it. It happened like this.

In the final week of September 1973 I felt an urge to go off on my own. I couldn't explain it to myself or Judy, but on Friday after work I packed a suitcase, got into my car, and told her I'd be back in a few days. I then drove east with no idea of where I was going or why. I drove until I ran smack into the Atlantic Ocean in Maine and then north to Portland, where I found a room for the night. I was exhausted and a little depressed. I didn't want to be in a strange hotel room by myself; I wanted to be home with Judy and the boys. The next morning I continued my feverish drive, still not knowing whether I was running from something or moving toward it. I saw a sign to Montreal and headed northwest. At dusk I was driving past a lake. Although a part of me wanted to keep going to reach Montreal, where there would be lights and people, where I wouldn't be alone, another part, wise and gentle, told me I must stop. This is where I was to spend the night. I followed a dirt road which led to the lake. There along the shore were about a dozen cabins. Next to the parking lot was a dock with a few rowboats and canoes. I walked into the first cabin, which had a sign, OFFICE, over the door. Inside an older couple were watching a small TV. Yes, they said, I could rent a cabin for the night. "Can I take out a canoe?" I asked. Yes, the boats and canoes were for the guests.

I paddled hard, wanting to reach the center of the lake while there was still light to see. At first I heard nothing but my own heart pounding. Then an "ooouuu ooouuu," a bird's eerie laugh, and I saw four black loons gliding toward the shore. A V of ducks flew over me. I could hear their velvet wings softly pummeling the air. I did not see them land but heard their splash. It was dark now. I could no longer see the shore. A mist of blackness had come off the water like a fog. I put my paddle into the canoe, closed my eyes, and listened. I waited to hear a duck quack or a loon cry or even the wind. But there was nothing.

I thought: I am alone. If I were to fall into the water and drown, no one would know. I felt a shiver of fear. It passed through me like a vapor. Warm again, I waited. Silence. Eyes open or closed, I saw the speckled light of blackness.

Then it happened. All of the people who I was began to leave me. Parts of me literally and physically, for I could feel my body being diminished, fell away, as if I were a snake shedding its layers of dead skin. Son, gone. Husband, gone. Father, gone. Lawyer, brother, friend, all gone. As these selves peeled away, I descended into an even deeper blackness, spiraling down and down, as if I were on a corkscrew. I was afraid, for I thought I must be dying. When all my selves are gone, what will be felt? What will be left? I wanted to open my eyes, make a sound, paddle toward the shore. I watched the urge die away and momentarily felt at peace. Then terror struck me like a storm. Almost to the bottom! Almost gone! And there will be nothing! Nothing! This agonizing fear lasted but a minute but its white-hot intensity cauterized my soul. I had no more selves to bleed. Gone. Nothing, nothing. I am nothing. Then thought fell away. And I was truly absolutely nothing.

I—My Ego—Dissolved, Yet I Continued to Be

But—and this is the mystery and the miracle—I did not die. I did not disappear. When I was gone, something else remained. It seems impossible to describe. An awareness, but not an awareness of any thing or any thought, just an awareness. It wasn't thin or ephemeral. The opposite. It was solid and strong and real. It seemed to have no boundaries.

The next thing I knew I was crying. I wept in gratitude and relief. Everything I am was gone, yet I continued to be. At first I had no words for it. And then: I am. I am. And these I did not speak but breathed. When the world stops—all sounds and all sights and all perceptions and finally all thoughts—and you remain to witness it, I tell you it's a miracle.

I paddled the canoe toward shore, rejoicing, first in the holy silence, and then in the words: I am. I am. I am.

I spent most of the night lying on the hard bed in the cabin, wide awake. I listened to the wind and to the soft, rhythmic sound of the water washing the shore. I thought about the experience in the canoe and understood why I had felt impelled to leave home. The experience reminded me of my earlier revelation, but this time there were no words, no explanations. I tried to understand, but how could I? I was a person, a human being with a particular history, separate and unique. But I was also the lake and the wind and the sky and the stars. I was everything. And I knew that this part of me was eternal and indestructible. It would never die.

I am. I am. How could I not think of the Old Testament God? Yahweh. *I Am Who Am.*

CHAPTER 13

A Visit to a Spiritualist Church

The small white church, a simple frame building with stained-glass windows, was ordinary and the people inside, much to my disappointment, did not look strange. I stood for a few seconds just inside the door and watched them—about sixty men and women, a few children—sitting reverently still, some turning pages of the thick red hymnals. A large black sign in the front of the church had posted three white numbers and 71 was on top. Beyond the sign I saw Jesus, looking younger and more optimistic than I remembered Him, still wearing the golden halo, staring down at me from His place on the front wall. There were no candles burning in the red glasses, no statues of Mary and the saints. A faint smell of furniture polish came off the dark-stained oak pews. I sat in the aisle seat in the last row and tried to look as solemn and churchlike and ordinary as the other people. But no matter how they looked, I knew they weren't ordinary. They believed in ghosts, spooks, apparitions. This was a Spiritualist church in conservative Albany, New York, where, rumor had it, the minister addressed not only God but the dead, who came to pass on messages to the living.

I said I didn't believe in ghosts, even as a child. Hadn't I made midnight visits with my friends to cemeteries to prove it? Still, believing or not, I always felt sweat on my hands and hair raise off my neck when I stood beside the tombstones. And that's how I felt that Sunday evening, sitting in the Spiritualist church.

A man going heavy in his old age came from a door in back of the church and began to play soothing chords on a small organ. The twisted tufts of white hair bounced on his collar as he moved into a spirited version of the "Battle Hymn of the Republic." As His truth went marching on, the minister, a pleasant-looking woman in her mid-forties wearing a white robe, marched in. She opened the service with a prayer to Father-God and then the congregation sang hymn number 71. Once or twice I almost joined in. Her sermon, based on a passage from the New Testament, was gently spoken and evidenced an intelligence I hadn't expected to find. There were more hymns and prayers and finally the passing of a basket. So far it was a typical Protestant service, and I wondered if I had made a mistake in coming. But then the minister, standing on the small stage where she had conducted the service, said, "Anyone who has to leave the church during the next hour, please leave now. Communication with spirit is about to begin."

I was wire-tight. It's just a show, I told myself, trying to ignore the beat of my heart as it pounded the veins in my neck. I stared at the minister in an unseemly way, looked as hard as I could. Maybe I couldn't believe, but I could look. Her head dropped slowly down until her forehead rested on her palm. Then, moving just as slowly, her head raised and her eyes looked out beyond us. "It helps if everyone keeps his feet flat on the floor," she said. Her right arm shot out, pointing like an arrow to a woman in the right front of the church. "I come to you," said the minister, and the woman responded, "Thank you."

"I have here an elderly lady who I get the impression is on the maternal side of your family, your mother or grandmother. Her name—wait a minute now—" and now, though it was hard to believe my eyes, the minister turned 180 degrees and, speaking to the air between her and the potted plant by the wall, she said: "What's your name, honey—that's okay, take your time—Do you know a Lillian in spirit?"

"I have an aunt Lillian who died," whispers the woman.

"Well she's here. She says you've been worrying a lot—wait a

minute now, not too fast"—once again she turns toward the plant—
"you've been worrying about something you can't change. I don't
know what she's talking about, do you? Do you understand?"

The woman nods.

"Then I leave that with you. God bless," says the minister, raising
her arm in blessing to the woman and then pointing to a middle-aged
man on the other side of the aisle. "I come to you."

The man coughs nervously, bringing his hand to his mouth, and
responds with a muffled thank-you.

"Mr. Donnellson, your wife is here again." The minister now turns
and says to the plant or to the air or to Mrs. Donnellson, the spirit,
"Yes, dear, yes . . . okay . . . I'll tell him . . . don't worry." Facing
the man she says: "Your wife says you've been feeling badly again.
She wants you to know she's happy. She's watching over you and it
hurts her to see you upset . . . do you know what she is talking
about?"

"Yes," the man says. "Yes, I know. It's just I miss her." He starts
to speak, his voice breaks, he stops. A few seconds pass before he says,
"Tell her I love her."

The minister turns to Mrs. Donnellson. "You heard, he wants you
to know he loves you. Yes, I can tell him. Are you sure you want
me to tell him that? Okay." To Mr. Donnellson she says: "She wants
you to know that you're still her man and she's still as jealous as she
ever was."

The minister laughs, shakes her head; others laugh, too. "I'll leave
that with you. God bless." Her head now jumps to the back of the
church.

"Someone back there—I don't know who—do you have a mother
or grandmother in spirit who came from Germany?"

A thin man, red-haired and pale, sitting in my pew raises his hand.
"It could be my grandmother," he says.

The minister has turned her back to us again and is conversing with
Grandmother. "I'm sorry, but I don't speak German. No, you can't
borrow my voice. I don't do it that way. You tell me, I tell them."
She calls to the young man: "She doesn't speak English very well.
Hardly at all."

"She never did," he replies.

"Well, listen, dear, you get yourself a translator and come back.
No, I'm sorry. I said no!"

To the man: "If she gets herself a translator, I'll come back to you."

I Had to Return to the Spiritualist Church to Find Out What Was Happening

I went home that evening curiously relieved that the minister had not
called on me. As real as the communication with spirits seemed, I
could still dismiss the evening as a farce, a well-performed play, nothing more. But could I? Ghosts? Was the minister mad? Were they all
mad? She couldn't be doing it for the money. The silver and few dollar bills in the collection basket were hardly enough to heat the
church. What was going on? After thinking about it for a while, I
decided I would go back to try to find out.

Before I returned to the church, I read as much as I could about
spirits. I already knew what the good nuns had told me about the
children of Fatima, Bernadette of Lourdes, and others to whom
Sacred Spirits had appeared. As a child I had told the saints I wasn't
good enough—they shouldn't waste their time with me. In high
school the Christian Brothers were concerned with Basketball, Latin,
and Ejaculations (strange as the word is, what's stranger still is that
we never joked about the word, never thought it funny) like "Saint
John Baptist de la Salle, Pray for Us." Visions were rarely mentioned.
And at Fordham, the Jesuits would have laughed a spirit back into the
ground, having first impaled him on an Aristotelian syllogism. I
didn't come away from the Jesuits knowing much about spirits.
Because I didn't believe didn't mean I couldn't read about them, and
what I read really fascinated me.

Communication with spirit is as old as death. It has been practiced
by such diverse groups as the North American Indians and the !King
Zhu/Twasi of Botswana. But modern Spiritualism began in 1848 in
Hydesville, New York (Spiritualism, Mormonism, and Seventh Day
Adventism were founded within a fifteen-year period and within a

few miles of each other), when two young girls, Margaret and Kate Fox, understood the "rappings" in their family's farmhouse as a message from a dead soul. The Fox sisters established a code with the spirit, who identified himself as a man who had been murdered in the house. For some reason it gave me tremendous satisfaction to think about a spirit rapping out a message to two little girls.

The practice of communicating with spirits spread rapidly. The Fox sisters and other mediums gave sittings throughout the United States and England. Although many attended séances out of curiosity, there were those who had serious reasons to consult a medium: They sought evidence of human survival of bodily death, information about the future life, and, most important, consolation in believing they were able to communicate with relatives and loved ones on the other side. To promote these serious ends, Spiritualist associations and later churches were formed.

I returned to the small white church half a dozen times in the next few months. I was no longer tense—just the opposite—I felt calm and good being there. I never could bring myself to pray to Father-God, or even to let my mind go along with the minister's prayers, but I sang the hymns.

One evening a pony-tailed blond-haired woman in her late twenties received a message from her husband. The minister went on at length about how he was killed—shot by an assassin who was hiding behind a pillar of a large building. The husband scolded the woman for the way she was raising their son. "He's my kid, too, you know. He's getting out of hand. Gotta come down hard on him."

After the service I caught the woman outside the church. "Was it true?" I asked. "What she said about your husband."

"Oh yes. I guess I have been letting Stephen get away with things."

Mary Ellen Saw Spirits All the Time

The woman—her name was Mary Ellen—and I spent some time that evening talking about the spirit world. She saw spirits all the time. She was a medical secretary and gave reincarnation readings on the side. Although Mary Ellen claimed she didn't read books, she spoke intelligently about many things. While we were talking about the power of ideas, she said, "William James once said we must elevate ourselves with our words."

"Then you've read James?" I said.

"No, he told me that. He's one of the spirits I'm in contact with."

Another evening, after a Sunday service, Mary Ellen and I went to a coffee shop. No matter what we talked about, one of her spirit friends had a tidbit to add to the discussion. The constant interruption was annoying. More disturbing was the fact that their comments were appropriate and occasionally profound. When it was close to three A.M., the fatigue finally got to me. My eyes were closing. "I'm exhausted," I said.

The next thing I knew I felt a surge of energy unlike anything I ever felt before or since. It was as if a radio on low had been turned up full blast. My eyes sprung open. I felt as if I could leap across the room. I looked at Mary Ellen. Her eyes were closed and her face was knitted in deep concentration. She opened her eyes and said: "In a few minutes—"

"In a few minutes nothing! Christ, what did you do?"

"I have to be careful about how much power I send." She smiled. "I did it to my girlfriend once and she didn't sleep for two days."

I got home about three-thirty, but was wide awake until dawn.

Mary Ellen lived on the second floor of a two-family house over the doctor's office where she worked. I brought my brother there on a late Sunday evening for a reincarnation reading. We sat at her kitchen table where she and her best friend, Saint Francis of Assisi, whom she called Master Francis, often sat and talked about spiritual matters. (She told me this the night we met.) Mary Ellen cautioned us not to touch her while she was in a trance. She asked the Higher Powers to open the Akashic Records, her left hand and then her whole arm began to tremble, and her voice, husky and painful to my ears, described my brother's past lives. Three hours and twenty lives later Mary Ellen came out of her trance. My brother was pleased that he had been everything from a Tibetan lama, with a white beard and robe, to a soldier of fortune in sixteenth-century South America, where, according to Mary Ellen, he had made love to every woman he had gotten his hands on. My brother had always wanted to visit Africa, and so we were surprised when she told him: "You've always wanted to go to Africa. You will soon, and you'll find great peace there. The reason is you've lived many happy lives on that continent." (Ten months later a business trip brought my brother to northern Africa.)

I wasn't much interested in past lives, mine or anybody else's. I was more concerned with where I had lost my keys. I had checked house, office, car, everything; as of that morning I was locked out of the world, the only one I knew. The only question I had—the one I asked—was: "Mary Ellen, do you know where the hell my keys are?"

My Spirit Guides Were All Around Me

"Ask one of your spiritual guides," she said. "They're all around you tonight." And nodding to my left shoulder, she said, "There's an East Indian and an English doctor there, and over there"—pointing with her eyes over my right shoulder—"there's a Chinese monk wearing a white robe and an American Indian, and in back of them all there's an Inca Indian. Ask him."

I stood up, turned around, and, gritting my teeth out of anger, frustration, and intense disbelief, I looked, wanting to see, knowing I couldn't. But then, though I saw only the wall with my physical eyes, in my mind appeared an image of a little brown man wearing a dirty white loincloth, a gold amulet around his neck, and, of all things, golden slippers.

"What color slippers does he have on?" I said.

"Gold," Mary Ellen said, "and a gold ornament hanging around his neck. You see him, don't you?"

"I don't *see* anything," I said. "I have this image . . ."

"Ask him about the keys."

I didn't want to ask this mental creature, which I had obviously created, about anything, but I did. "Where are the keys?" I said aloud.

"In your bathroom," came his response as a thought.

"He says they're in my bathroom. Ridiculous!" Smart-faced, I turned to Mary Ellen: "I *never* go into the bathroom with my keys."

When I got home, I looked—I *had* to look—and sure enough the damn keys were in the bathroom on the brown wicker basket where we put the dirty clothes. I looked upward, inside my head, to see if the Inca was still around. I was relieved to find he was gone.

A Prophecy: I Would Meet My Spiritual Teacher

One Sunday at the Spiritualist church, the retired pastor, a tall, thin man who wore wire-rimmed glasses, called on me. What he told me was general: I was searching, I was interested in parapsychology; there was no message from "spirit." Several weeks later he called on me again and told me I would be taking a trip "to the west" which would be beneficial for me. (At the time I received the message, I was planning the Baltimore trip to see Mrs. Worrall.) He said that on my trip I would meet a "teacher." The teacher would be a lama from the Himalayas of Tibet. "But he's also a Christian. He's a tall man. You'll meet him in a churchlike structure."

When I made my trip to Baltimore, I did not know if this was the trip "to the west" that the minister had spoken of. Nor did I accept or reject the "truth" of the message about meeting a teacher. I was open to whatever might happen. After the Thursday morning healing service, as I described earlier, a luncheon was served in an adjoining building, part of the old church which had been renovated. I remember thinking at the time that the building could certainly be described as a "churchlike structure." I soon forgot the prophecy, for I was fascinated by Mrs. Worrall. After our discussion, I asked Mrs. Worrall where I might telephone for a taxi to take me to the railroad station. My question was overheard by a man who had come to say good-bye to her. He told me he was going in the direction of the station and would be glad to give me a lift.

Jim seemed like a pleasant man. He was about six years older than me, which made him about forty at the time we met. He was tall, with soft, inquisitive eyes. He was obviously Caucasian, but he also looked Middle Eastern. His skin was dark, and he had a strong patrician nose. In the car we talked about Mrs. Worrall and healing and then a little about ourselves. I learned that Jim was the chief psychologist for a major medical school and that he had come today with some of his psychiatric residents and a few children with cerebral palsy. When he told me this, I remembered seeing him at the beginning of the service, carrying a severely deformed child to Mrs. Worrall. Several young men—the residents, I realized—had carried other children to the altar so that Mrs. Worrall could hold them.

When Jim dropped me off at the station, I didn't think I'd be seeing him again. We hadn't talked about spiritual matters and I had no reason to believe he was a spiritual teacher. Before getting out of the car our easy conversation allowed me to ask about his parentage. He told me that one of his grandparents had been Samoan.

After I returned to Albany, I felt impelled to write him a letter of thanks for the ride to the station. I also sent a gift—a small seashell, beautifully designed by nature, from Samoa. I had written to him at the medical school, and he answered my letter, giving me his home address. This was the beginning of an intense correspondence that lasted many years.

As it turned out, Jim was a spiritual teacher. For years he had led spiritual discussion groups. He was thoroughly familiar with every religious and spiritual tradition. Whatever questions I asked he was able to answer in startling detail. Several times I visited him at his home, where we would talk almost nonstop for the weekend. Although it was clear that he had become my spiritual teacher, he preferred to be thought of as a spiritual co-worker.

The Hindus have a saying: The guest is God. And that is the way I felt whenever I was in Jim's house. He prepared delicious, wholesome meals, always beautifully presented. He gave me his time and wisdom freely. I never felt obligated to give him anything in return. He told me there were natural, spiritual laws that governed our relationship, laws that, in fact, required it.

How accurate had the minister's prophecy been? I knew Jim was a Christian. He believed that Jesus was an avatar, that is, an incarnation of God. He believed that God had appeared as man numerous times throughout history: as Zoroaster, Krishna, Buddha, Moham-

med, Jesus, and most recently as Meher Baba. Jim also remembered
his own past lives as a Tibetan lama. And so the minister's description
of Jim—as strange as it was—was valid in the sense that it matched
the way Jim identified himself.

CHAPTER 14

A Year in Florida

When Judy and I were married in 1965, she had a master's degree in child development. She supported us during our first year of marriage, working in a family therapy clinic while I attended law school. Except when the boys were infants and toddlers, she continued her career working with children and their families. In 1975 she decided to study for her doctorate in educational psychology and chose to work with Ira Gordon, who was a well-known researcher at the University of Florida. The timing was right. One of the properties I had an interest in was sold. The proceeds yielded an income sufficient to support us. I was working for a New York State Supreme Court justice as his law clerk. Although the job had no public status and was considered a dead-end position for a lawyer, it was exactly what I needed. I worked in the judge's library, doing research and writing memoranda. I made my own hours. The job was absolutely stress-free. I arranged with my boss, with whom I had a good relationship, to take a one-year leave of absence.

We rented our house in Albany and I went to Gainesville in the summer to rent a house for September. One of the last things I had to do before moving to Florida was to go to the medical center for my six-month checkup. I was ambivalent. Since I was holding firmly to the conviction I was cured, I didn't feel the need for the doctor's confirmation. Moreover, despite my knowing attitude, the visits were always stressful. They stirred up the old emotions—fear, anger, resentment—that I tried to avoid or transcend. I doubted. I worried.

I still have a memory-scar of my last visit to the oncology clinic.

139

The wait for my name to be called seemed endless; it lasted for over an hour. Finally the nurse called my name so loudly that I felt it could be heard outside the hospital walls. I tried to excuse her behavior. She was young, insensitive. Certainly she did not intend to injure me, and I should not think—as I did—that I'd like to kill her. She took several vials of blood from my arm. This was something new and I asked her why she needed so much blood.

"Because we can run as many as five [maybe it was ten] different tests to see if there's any disease in you," she replied enthusiastically. "We can tell if there's anything wrong with your liver, we can tell if—"

I tuned her out. She no longer existed.

A young doctor, one whom I had never seen before, came in and did some superficial probing with his fingers. Within a few minutes he was gone and I was getting dressed. I knew I would never come back.

In Florida my primary role was househusband. Chris was eight and Dave, six. Judy would get up early with the boys and get them breakfast. Then she'd go off on her bicycle to the university for the day. I slept late—until nine or ten. It was a period in my life in which I had a significant number of dreams each morning. If I didn't have my dreams, I was usually out of sorts the rest of the day. When the boys came home about three, I gave them a snack, talked with them. I would do the shopping, prepare the evening meal, do the dishes. The role change was initially confusing for the boys. When they came home from school, they would often say, "Hi, Mom," as they walked in the door.

I spent much of my spare time writing and, just as important to me, living the life of a writer. I had met Harry Crews, a fine novelist and a full professor in the English department of the University of Florida, at the Breadloaf Writers' Conference in 1973. Harry allowed me to attend his creative writing classes, where we discussed short stories and talked about the nuts and bolts of writing fiction. After class I would sometimes join him and a few students to have a drink and trade stories. Harry was often on assignment to write feature articles for *Playboy* and *Esquire*, and it was always exciting to hear him describe his journalistic exploits.

Fascination With Spiritual Matters Persists

My interest in Spiritualism and spiritual issues continued while I was in Florida. On a number of occasions I visited Cassadega, a Spiritualist community about two hours south of Gainesville. It's an old town with about a hundred houses on small winding streets. Many of these houses have signs in the windows: CERTIFIED MEDIUM, CERTIFIED HEALER. I don't know whether it's the gray strands of Spanish moss hanging from the giant live oaks and pines that makes the town seem so eerie or just the signs in the windows, but as soon as you enter you know this town is different in an unsettling way. Most of the people in the town are Spiritualists, or if they don't admit to that, they might say, as the English lady who ran the grocery store told me, "I'm not one of them, but I believe in metaphysics."

On one of my visits I learned the tenets of the church. They're quite simple: There is no dogma or creed as such, just a Declaration of Principles, nine altogether. Spiritualists believe in "Infinite Intelligence," a supreme Impersonal Power that manifests itself as life. They affirm that the existence and personal identity of the individual continue after death and that communication with the so-called dead is a fact, scientifically proven by the phenomenon of Spiritualism. The highest morality is contained in the Golden Rule. They affirm the moral responsibility of the individual—he makes his own happiness or unhappiness as he obeys or disobeys Nature's physical and spiritual laws. And the doorway to reformation is never closed, here or hereafter—there's no such thing as eternal damnation.

I enjoyed walking the streets of Cassadega, talking to the residents and occasionally attending a service, but I never thought of becoming a Spiritualist. I simply wanted to be exposed to new experiences and new ideas. Similarly, I was learning a great deal from Jim, my spiritual teacher whom I had met in Baltimore, but what he taught me didn't become part of my belief system. I needed to have my beliefs based upon my own experience, not on what someone told me. And so on an intellectual level, Jim's teaching was merely information. But on another level I believe I was attaching myself to his basic cosmology.

Everything Is Part of God

In pre-creation "time" only God existed, but this God was not self-aware. Because God wanted to know Himself—the divine whim—He manifested Himself externally by creating the universe. Every element of the physical universe, then, is a part of God. Each element from the beginning of creation had a form of consciousness. The primordial mixture of gases that formed the universe was in some sense "conscious," as were all the subsequent elements in the evolutionary chain: rock, water, air, earth, plants, animals. At some place in the process of evolution, the "consciousness" became individualized. Each person has an individual soul and that soul always existed, first as a part of the Unconscious God, and then as part of the evolving universe.

The purpose of creation is self-knowledge. In order for that knowledge to be complete, each element of the original Unconscious God must come to the realization, the experiential realization, that he (or she or it) is God. This knowing is called God-realization or self-realization.

Since each of us began his individual existence as inorganic matter, we have all lived millions of lifetimes. And our lifetimes—reincarnations—will continue until our own individual God-realization occurs.

The first being who completed this journey of spiritual evolution did not remain aloof from the process of others' spiritual progress. His task was and is to help all of us become God-realized. And so He and others who have become illumined work unceasingly to help us in our spiritual growth, to help us toward our goal. At particular times in history the first God-man has found it necessary to be born again and to live the life of a human. Thus the avatars of the ages (to name a few): Zoroaster, Krishna, Buddha, Jesus, Mohammed, and recently Meher Baba.

Most of humanity live their lives completely bound in illusion, identifying with their bodies and minds, but not their spirits or their souls. It's a huge leap forward for one to even begin his journey on the spiritual path, which has six distinct planes or stages. The seventh plane is Reality Itself, and entrance into this stage of spiritual development ends the First Divine Journey. But even God-realization is not static: The journey continues to even higher levels of realization.

Jim never recommended books for me to read except at my urging. At his suggestion I read the works of Meher Baba, particularly *God Speaks* and his three-volume *Discourses*. I also read a number of spiritual books on my own, the most memorable being Paramahansa Yogananda's *Autobiography of a Yogi*. In that book Yogananda described events—miracles!—which ordinarily I would have dismissed as fantasy. But for some reason I never doubted the truth of what the saintly man wrote.

Transpersonal Psychology Changed My Life

Perhaps my most important discovery in Florida—for it changed the direction of my life—was the field of transpersonal psychology. I came across a copy of the *Journal of Transpersonal Psychology* in the library. When I read the statement of purpose of the journal, I had a feeling of coming home.

> The Journal of Transpersonal Psychology is concerned with the publication of theoretical and applied research, empirical papers, articles and studies in transpersonal process, values and states, unitive consciousness, meta-needs, peak experiences, ecstasy, mystical experience, being, essence, bliss, awe, wonder, transcendence of self, spirit, sacralization of everyday life, oneness, cosmic awareness, cosmic play, individual and species-wide synergy, the theories and practices of meditation, spiritual paths, compassion, transpersonal cooperation, transpersonal realization and actualization; and related concepts, experiences and activities.

My interest in spiritual matters had a name; it had a subject matter, a body of knowledge. It was a field I could pursue.

The Maharaj-ji Was Cool

The most memorable event that occurred in Florida was my visit to
see the boy guru, Maharaj-ji, who I had read about in the newspaper
on a number of occasions. He was scheduled to give a talk at a lake
outside of Orlando. I drove down with a few friends from Gainesville
to hear what he had to say. I was amazed to see how large the crowd
was. Over ten thousand people had gathered around the lake in a
semicircle. The Maharaj-ji, who was around sixteen or seventeen at
the time, spoke from a large boat in the center of the lake. It was a
beautiful day. The sun was shining and the sky was cloudless. The
people listened with reverence. Most of them were obviously his fol-
lowers. I was not particularly impressed with his words. He spoke the
usual religious bromides: God is love; we are all children of God; we
must love each other as God loves us.

What happened while he spoke I will never forget. I happened to
look over my shoulder and saw a cloud about a thousand feet in the
air moving in our direction. But it was not an ordinary cloud. It spar-
kled with bits of luminescent light: greens and blues and other colors.
And it was shaped—distinctly shaped—in the form of an arrow. The
point of the arrow was heading towards Maharaj-ji. Other people saw
the cloud, and the air was suddenly filled with the buzz of thousands
of excited voices. When the cloud reached the lake and began to pass
over the boat, there was a collective gasp. Then silence. The
Maharaj-ji had noticed the cloud. What would he say?

Now I know I would have said something like, Well, that proves
it, folks: Let that be a sign unto you. Something! But the boy guru,
if nothing else, was cool. He just chuckled and continued his talk. He
had been talking about God manifesting Himself in the world in different forms, in different ways. He had mentioned Jesus. As the cloud
passed over his head, he said, "God has come to us before, and He
will come to us again."

That evening I wrote to Jim, telling him what I had witnessed. His
reply was sobering. He reminded me of something he had told me
before: that psychic and occult phenomena were not necessarily spiritually significant. He knew people who were fully capable of altering

the weather who were not spiritually developed. A genuine guru or saint might sometimes display these powers but it was rare. In general, psychic gifts were not a manifestation of spirituality.

CHAPTER 15

Unfulfilled Dreams: Becoming a Psychotherapist

A s I mentioned earlier, my desire to become a psychotherapist began when I was eighteen, a college freshman, because of my mother's mental illness. The little boy in me wanted to save her, and if not her, then people like her. In order to pursue my interest in psychology I had transferred from Georgetown to Fordham in the middle of my sophomore year. I had kept my desire to become a psychologist a secret from my father as long as I could. Then I had entered a doctoral program and had quit before the semester was over. Now, almost twenty years later, I decided to study for a master's degree in clinical and transpersonal psychology at a university in California.

A More Intimate Engagement

I had been mulling over the possibility for over a year. One of Jim's questions to me had been, "Now that you're cured, what are you going to do with the rest of your life?" It was not a question he expected me to answer but to think about. I knew

146

I was ready to come out of the sanctuary of the law library. I wanted to engage people, not as a lawyer, but in a deeper, more intimate way.

I chose John F. Kennedy University in Orinda, just east of Berkeley, because of its program in consciousness studies. It also had what appeared to be a fine clinical program in its psychology department with an emphasis on teaching both the theory and practice of psychotherapy. The joint degree program—transpersonal and clinical psychology—would take two years.

Judy and the boys were very supportive. They all looked forward to this new adventure. I gave my boss about six months notice that I would be leaving—this time for good.

The most difficult part of the decision was telling my father. He had long ago accepted the fact that I would never practice law with him, but I was still a source of pride. I was a lawyer. My brother and I went to see him weekly for an evening of cards. How could I tell him I would be leaving? He was eighty-one. I might not see him again. I had no discomfort when I imagined telling my mother. She would say, "Do what's best for you." But my father would be angry and hurt. It was my task, or so I perceived it then, to protect my father from pain. I should never be the source of it. The child inside me did not want to risk a rupture in our relationship—whatever that relationship was. When I found myself literally unable to tell my father I was leaving law, leaving to live in California for two years, I entered therapy. After four months, I was able to break the news. He did not rant or rave as I expected but shook his head, unable to comprehend my reasons. "You're lost," he said. "You're at sea." Then we continued the card game and nothing further was said.

In 1977 we had moved into a new suburban development because we wanted to live in a neighborhood where there were more children for our kids to play with. It was a new house. When we made our move to California in the summer of 1978, we had no trouble renting it. We drove to California in our station wagon, taking the southern route (a mistake, for we had no air conditioning), and rented an unfurnished house in Walnut Creek. We furnished the house with garage-sale bargains. The newest member of our family, Samantha, a black Labrador retriever, stayed temporarily with—who else?—Robert Young in Washington. He arranged to fly her to San Francisco. The family intact, our new life began.

My two years in California were exciting and rich, filled with new experiences. My return to student status at the age of thirty-seven was not stressful. Most of the other students were beginning their second or third careers. We had teachers, businesspeople and artists, and a psychiatrist in the program. We were kindred spirits, wanting to learn more about the spiritual dimension, wanting to grow in that area and to help others as therapists.

We took basic graduate courses in the psychology department: theories of therapy and personal growth, basic counseling skills, theories of psychopathology, Gestalt therapy, marriage and family counseling, human sexuality. The courses in transpersonal psychology tended to be more esoteric: theory and practice of transpersonal process (the experiential and theoretical exploration of methods of working with people that facilitate physical, emotional, mental, and spiritual growth and wholeness); issues in body/mind/spirit interaction (the study of the mind-body therapies such as Alexander technique, Polarity therapy, aikido, tai chi, bioenergetics, and Rolfing); spiritual psychologies and the nature of man (clinical implications of various spiritual systems, including Zen Buddhism, Sufism, Christian mysticism, Hasidism, Taoism, and Yoga).

My Professors' Openness Taught Me it Was All Right to Reveal Myself

Our professors were generally experienced practitioners. They often exhibited an openness I had never seen before. Their self-disclosures were not gratuitous but were made to illustrate a point or to put flesh on an abstract discussion. For example, one professor told us of his experience as a manic-depressive. He sometimes cried in class. Another, who taught a course on Jung, told us about his relationship with his son when we were discussing parenting. A third described the grief of his divorce when the topic was transient depression. What the professors did, besides give information, was to model for us that they were, first and foremost, human beings, not teachers or therapists but people who, like us, had personal lives filled with problems and projects, dreams and fears, hopes and memories, both happy and sad. It was not a spoken message, but one clearly sent: This is who I am; it is all right for you to reveal who you are, too.

Self-revelation required a vocabulary I was not conversant with, the vocabulary of feelings. Of course I knew the words: anger, fear, sadness, joy, rage, and so forth. But I often had trouble identifying the words with my own experience. In group process classes, the questions were often asked, "What are you experiencing right now? What physical sensations? What feelings? What are you thinking?" I could readily answer the last question, but the others would often elicit nothing, an I-don't-know. I was not the only one with the problem. Our group process class was generally divided between the thinkers and the feelers. We thinkers were always "in our heads"—we would give opinions, we would say "I think such and such." The feelers, on the other hand, were always emoting, and they would often get damn angry with the often intellectual, arid, passionless responses of the thinkers. In response to these attacks I began to feel frustrated and then angry and then—eureka!—I was able to identify emotional experiences as they began to occur. In looking back, I believe one of the most important things I learned was about feelings—mine and others.

As I try to recall the many rich experiences during that two years I think first of Esalen. I knew it was the Mecca of the New Age movement, where legendary figures such as Fritz Perls, the founder of Gestalt therapy, had spent time giving workshops. I had also heard it was a beautiful place situated on a peninsula, overlooking the Pacific. Judy and I chose to spend a weekend there in a workshop with Gregory Bateson. It was a heady experience. Bateson was clearly a genius, and listening to him—focusing with all the concentration I could muster—forced my mind to take giant steps, then leaps, into the intellectual ether. At times he spoke very personally— once again that openness, that self-revelation, I saw in my teachers at school. He had lung cancer. He knew he was dying. He wondered if his contribution had been significant, if his life had mattered. I remember thinking at the time: My God, this man's work has left its mark on so many disciplines—psychology, psychiatry, education, philosophy, anthropology—if his life had no consequence, whose does? His self-doubt—and his dying, for that matter—did not evoke pity. He seemed too big for that, too wise.

The physical beauty of Esalen had been understated. The views of the ocean below, the waves crashing on the rocks, and the mountains behind were awesome. Men, women, children swam naked in the swimming pool. Vegetable and flower gardens abounded. I had my first massage. It was given with extraordinary tenderness and skill. I had never felt my body so deeply, so deliciously. As I lay there marveling at the plethora of new sensations, I began to dream.

That night Judy and I sat in one of the hot sulfur baths which are on a ledge overlooking the ocean and watched one of the most star-filled skies I had ever seen. We listened to the waves lapping over the rocks in the distance. This is the Garden of Eden, I thought. This is paradise.

Patricia Sun's Extraordinary Sounds Produced Rapture

The School of Consciousness Studies at JFK often brought in guest speakers. One evening Olga Worrall lectured on psychic healing and described some scientific studies which verified that the energy sent through her hands could alter microorganisms in a petri dish under controlled laboratory conditions. On another occasion Patricia Sun was scheduled to appear, and I was told by some fellow students that her talk was something I shouldn't miss. She was an attractive woman, tall, with long blond hair. She was intelligent—a Ph.D. psychologist—and articulate. Her topic was the healing power of love. Her warmth and wit were endearing and I would have been satisfied if the evening had ended with her lecture. But it didn't. She asked us—about a hundred people in the hall—to get comfortable. I forget how she described what she was about to do, but it had something to do with sound. I closed my eyes and then opened them and waited. Suddenly the air was filled with the most unusual sound I had ever heard. It was a woman's voice—Patricia Sun's—singing in a high register, a perfect pitch. The sound grew stronger, higher, more perfect. I experienced joy, then rapture. Then, even more strange, the cells in my head realigned themselves. That is the only way I can describe it. The left side and the right side of my brain felt attuned, balanced. I wish I could be more precise, but I felt a definite physical shifting inside my head that made me feel better, more centered, more whole. After she left the podium, I compared notes with some friends. They had had similar reactions to Patricia Sun's extraordinary sounds.

A month into the program the thirty or so students in our class went on a retreat to a spiritual center in northern California known for its mineral water baths and pools. About midnight, after most of the other students had retired, I was sitting with a newfound friend, Jim Van Dyk, an artist and teacher, who had come from Vermont to study in the program. We were communing with the full moon, the planets, the starry heavens, and the dark, mystifying silence of the earth when the energy changed. Not just California talk. I'm talking about the air thickening, the wind coming up and hissing in the trees, birds squawking. I thought that by some strange quirk in the weather, a storm was descending. Then we heard the sound of running feet and saw the stampede of naked men and women who came out of the night, laughing and howling as they jumped into the swimming pool filled with warm mineral water. Jim and I watched as speechless as we had been gazing at the infinitude of stars. The men and women were kissing, hugging, fondling each other. They were pairing off. They were screwing! Women shrieked and men shouted their orgasms into the sacred sky. Awe. Wonder. Cosmic play. Was this transpersonal psychology? I jumped into the pool and realized these weren't our fellow students. A yet unpaired woman told me they were members of a sexual encounter workshop designed to help people obtain release from repressive sexual inhibitions. That evening they had learned to touch and kiss each other—women and women,

men and men, it was all the same. The workshop was over for the evening. This was free time. And only Friday! What will they be doing by Sunday? I wondered. A man—my informant told me he was the workshop leader—was performing cunnilingus underwater on one of his pupils, his long nose serving as periscope. "Isn't he marvelous?" she asked. But I was already retreating from the pool. Jim and I left them laughing and moaning and walked to our rooms. Instead of "good night" I said, "Welcome to California."

The openness of both the professors and students at JFK allowed me to speak, for the first time really, about my illness. The only persons I remember telling before were my spiritual teacher, Jim, and Harry Crews. One evening in a process class of about fifteen students I told them what had happened to me. As I recalled the fear and sadness during that part of my life I wept openly. When I got to the point where I described the recurrence and the voice which had told me that I must know I was well, I really broke down. This time the release of tears was an expression of deep gratitude.

The professors often had a favorite story to tell, sometimes personal, sometimes not. I want to mention two of them here because both, in their own way, made significant impressions on me. The first was told by the professor with manic-depression. One day he and his wife were attending a Pirandello play at the Berkeley Auditorium. It was a black-tie optional affair, and Martin, let's call him, was wearing a tuxedo. Near the end of the first act, one actor, the stage manager in the play within the play, was addressing the audience. Martin felt an urge to get up from his seat and walk onto the stage. He told us that when he got urges like that he always checked with his wife to see if they should be expressed or suppressed. She said it would be all right for him to walk onto the stage. Martin rose from his seat, walked up the aisle, and found an entrance to the stage. As he walked to the center, the actor stopped speaking. Martin said in a loud voice to the audience, "I have come to take my bow." He then bowed deeply and the audience responded with a standing ovation.

I had been taught, as I believe most of us are, to be humble, to deny the existence of that part of me that wants to be acknowledged as special, that wants to be praised, even applauded. And here was Martin telling the class that this secret yearning wasn't shameful. It was human, it was good. "I'd rather be crazy," he'd often say, "and be *alive*, be able to *feel*, than walk around, as most people do, half-dead."

The other story is a Sufi tale told to us by one of our psychology profs, an experienced teacher and therapist who had been an early student of Fritz Perls. It's a story I've often repeated to friends and, most important, to myself.

A farmer in ancient China was considered most fortunate by his neighbors because he was the only farmer who owned a horse. All the other farmers had to plow their fields by hand. When they told him how lucky he was, he would shrug and say, "Maybe." One day, the horse ran away. The neighbors came to his house to express their sympathy. "What a shame," they said. "You've suffered such a great loss." Again the farmer shrugged and said, "Maybe." A few days later the horse returned, bringing with him a herd of wild horses. Now the neighbors came and told the farmer he must be the luckiest man in the empire. The farmer smiled and said, "Maybe." It was harvesttime and the farmer relied upon his only son for help. One day, while the son was breaking one of the wild horses, he fell and broke his leg. The neighbors shook their heads, saying surely the farmer was an unfortunate man. Predictably, the farmer replied, "Maybe." A few days later the emperor's soldiers arrived and conscripted all the young men in the area to fight in a war. The farmer's son, because of his broken leg, was not taken. Now the neighbors, in their sadness, gathered around the farmer and told him he was blessed. "Maybe," he replied. "Maybe."

Can We Deeply Feel Life's Joys and Sorrows and Simultaneously Be Detached?

I try to reconcile what Martin taught with the Sufi tale and, of course, I can't. How can one feel deeply life's joys and sorrows and at the same time say, "maybe"? How can one be fully engaged, fully committed, whether to a dream, career, or to another human being, or even to life in general, and simultaneously remain detached from the outcome of that engagement? Each viewpoint has its own wisdom, its own truth. Instead of choosing one or the other, I do what is most natural for me. I try to accept the paradox—the paradox of our nature—and choose both.

Judy spent much of that first academic year in California preparing to defend her dissertation. In July 1979 we flew to Florida to spend the month so she could consult with her committee.

In the fall I began seeing clients. First one, then two, and finally three people came to my house once a week. They understood I was a student and paid no fee. Doing therapy for me was a natural process. I listened well, empathized easily, and was able, I believe, to restate the client's problems in new ways so that awareness was deepened. I believed then—and still do—that the client knows more about him or herself than I could ever know and that my job was not to offer solutions. Rather, I was there to help facilitate a client's self-healing, to create a nurturing atmosphere in which that process could occur.

I had excellent supervision. Dr. Vera Fryling, a psychiatrist from Oakland and an expert on autogenics, a relaxation technique, was my individual supervisor. We talked weekly about my cases. In addition, about ten of us would meet with a faculty member for three hours a week of group supervision.

During the first year at JFK I had read a book for one of my classes—*Psychosynthesis* by Roberto Assagioli—which had such a strong influence on me that it led me to alter my direction. The book described Assagioli's system of psychology, which he had formulated in the early 1900s. Assogioli had been one of the founders of the psychoanalytic movement in Italy. He soon went beyond psychoanalysis and began to explore what Abraham Maslow, some sixty years later, would call "the farther reaches of human nature." Assagioli's purpose was to create a scientific approach that encompassed the whole person: creativity and will, joy and wisdom, as well as impulses and drives. And he wanted this integrative approach to be practical—not merely an understanding of how we live, but an aid in helping us live better, more fully, according to the best that is within each of us.

After finishing the book, I learned that there was an institute in San

Francisco that applied the principles of psychosynthesis to therapy. The training program was rigorous. I would take at least six hours of class a week and there would be plenty of homework. I applied and was accepted into the program. I was now, in effect, in three programs: the clinical program within the psychology department at JFK; the transpersonal program in the School of Consciousness Studies; and now the training program at the Synthesis Graduate School. I realized it would be impossible for me to pursue all of them and so, with some regret, I dropped out of the transpersonal program at Kennedy.

Psychosynthesis is, in fact, one of many transpersonal psychologies. In his book, *Transpersonal Psychologies*, Charles Tart points out that there are psychologies that are integral parts of various spiritual disciplines. Thus, Zen Buddhism has a psychology, as does Yoga, Christianity, and Sufism. Tart went on to say that these psychologies are working bodies of knowledge which, to some extent, can be looked at independently of the religious belief system ordinarily associated with them.

Psychosynthesis—A Therapeutic System With Spiritual Perspective

Psychosynthesis did not come out of a specific religious tradition, but it does have a definite spiritual perspective. It posits the essential unity of everything in creation and asserts there is a natural movement or evolution toward perfection. It states that all of us, though individual in form, partake in the same divine essence, which it calls *Soul* and which others might call God. As a psychological system, psychosynthesis has models or ways to describe reality. When I first read about these models, I was sympathetic to them because they were generally consistent with my own experience or intuition. The most central paradigm is the personality, which is thought of as a constellation of subpersonalities, having a center or seat of consciousness called the "I."

The subpersonalities are semi-autonomous parts of ourselves that are usually expressed in the various roles we play. For example, I might behave and experience myself one way as a father, another as a husband, another as a friend, and another associated with a professional role. In addition, we are said to have parts or subselves that correspond to the numerous psychological constellations that exist in all of us. We may have a spiritual part, call it the Mystic; a bitchy part, the Hag or the Grump; the Frightened Child (fairly common); the Pillar of Strength; the Doubter; the Critic. The cast of possible characters is endless. At any given point of time, we are experiencing the world through one of our subpersonalities. Some of them are the stars and take center stage much of the time, while others are waiting in the wings, undeveloped, wanting to speak a few lines, to be heard.

The center of one's personal being, the "I," has two functions or aspects: pure awareness and willing. The "I" is contentless. The experience of being simply "I" is rare, because we are usually experiencing ourselves through one of our subpersonalities. Or, at the least, we are identifying with what we are feeling or thinking. Psychosynthesis teaches that although we have sensations in our bodies, we are not our bodies. We have feelings, but we are not our feelings. And we have thoughts, but we are not our thoughts. To experience oneself separate from one's thoughts is quite interesting and not difficult to achieve. One can simply "watch" the mind as it produces thoughts. One then experiences a part of oneself—the watcher—as separate from one's thoughts. I learned an interesting trick to trigger the experience. Simply say to your mind, "Stop! I'm listening." A silence will usually follow and then you can observe your thoughts as they are being born.

As I became familiar with the psychosynthesis model, I thought of my experience at the lake when parts of myself (subpersonalities) seemed to dissolve, and for a moment I was both nothing and everything. In psychosynthesis terms this was an experience of the "I"—an experience of pure awareness.

I took classes at the Synthesis Graduate School for over a year. I became, I believe, a proficient "guide"—the name psychosynthesis gives to its therapists. At the end of my two-year stay in California

I felt I was well on my way to becoming a competent psychothera-pist.

Ken Keyes Emanates a Dazzling Light from His Triumphant Spirit

I can't close this period of my life without describing my meeting with a most extraordinary human being. I had driven down to Asilomar, a conference center south of San Francisco, to attend the Association for Transpersonal Psychology annual convention. At dinner I found myself sitting next to a kind-looking man with soft, sensitive eyes. He was sitting in a wheelchair. He fed himself slowly. He asked who I was, what I did, and within minutes we were engrossed in an animated conversation, sharing common interests and values. The meal was almost over before I realized the man I was speaking with was Ken Keyes, author of numerous books, including *The Handbook to Higher Consciousness*, which has sold nearly a million copies.

What I found extraordinary about Ken was that right after meeting him I forgot he was handicapped. He was so engaging that I lost the perception that he was in any way impaired. That he sat in a wheel-chair and had limited use of his hands seemed to be an insignificant detail of his life. When this realization struck me, I asked him how he really felt. He replied that although life in a wheelchair was not one that he would have chosen and that he would have preferred it another way, still his situation did not affect his ability to live a happy, satisfying life.

Other people also seemed to quickly forget or even not to notice that Ken was handicapped. The next day while I was walking down a path I saw a group gathered around him. Ken was being asked to autograph copies of his book by these admirers. Writing was a slow, arduous process for him, but no one seemed uncomfortable watching him. I don't believe they were insensitive. For them, as well as for me, it was difficult, almost impossible, to think of Ken Keyes in any way but whole and perfect.

Ken Keyes remains vivid in my memory: a warm, contented, life-loving human being. When I think of him, I am still dazzled by the brilliant light of his triumphant spirit.

CHAPTER 16

Unfulfilled Dreams: Becoming a Stand-Up Comic

I have mentioned my belief, shared by others who have written on the subject, that the will to live is an important element in getting well. Some people I know seem attached to life because they find it delightful and delicious. They may have some ambition, but they don't live to achieve. They find satisfaction in simply being alive.

But these people, in my experience, are rare. Most people I know—I, among them—have defined life-goals. When I was a child, I was told by my Catholic teachers that everyone has a vocation—a calling by God to do something important with his life. Although my primary goals—what I think of as vocations—were to become a writer and a psychotherapist, I had other dreams as well.

Becoming a Stand-Up Comic Was a Tantalizing Dream

My most enduring fantasy—it began in my early twenties and lasted for nearly two decades—was to be a stand-up comic. As fantasies go, it was on a par with my desire to make love to Sophia Loren. The chance of it happening was not simply improbable—it was clearly impossible. But that didn't stop me from dreaming. In fact, in both cases the impossibility of the dream allowed the fantasy to become deeper and richer because the restraints of reality were completely absent. My thoughts of Ms. Loren did not even impinge on my Catholic conscience, which proscribed committing adultery in my heart. After all, I wasn't *serious*.

I wasn't serious about doing stand-up comedy, either, because of who I was—or more accurately, because of who I perceived myself to be. I've come to believe that self—who I really am—and self-perception are for practical purposes one and the same. I thought of myself as a shy, reticent person. I grew up a loner, an introvert. I had difficulty connecting with people in easy conversation. I was not the class clown, never even thought of auditioning for a part in the school play. As a lawyer I had never tried a case, because standing up in front of a jury would have engendered more anxiety than I was willing to bear. But I enjoyed humor, particularly stand-up comics. I went to see Mort Sahl and Dick Gregory in the early sixties. Buddy Hackett, Bill Cosby, Johnny Carson, Woody Allen, Jonathan Winters, Robin Williams, Jay Leno—I love them all. I never thought for a second that I would do anything but watch. My fantasy would always be . . . just a fantasy.

When I was living in Florida in 1975, I read an article in the *Gainesville Sun* about a woman—she was a lawyer and probably cooked and scrubbed floors, too, so that I could easily identify with her—whose dream was to be a stand-up comic. That was it. She had come out of the closet with her dream, a reporter had written a story about her, and the *Sun*, in bad need of local news, I supposed, had printed it. But that story, as insignificant as it might appear, altered my perception of what was possible and thus changed my life.

What the woman said in the interview was that she would perform at the comedy club that had just opened in Gainesville—if she had just ten minutes of good material. Ten minutes was all. I thought: If I had ten good minutes, would I do it? Before I could answer the question I found myself in conversation with the faceless lawyer, telling her she was full of beans. She didn't have the guts to stand up on a stage and say, in effect, to the audience: I'm going to make you laugh. I realized I was talking to myself and responded: Damn right. I'm not nuts.

But her thought—what I considered mad bravado—seized me. Maybe she was telling the truth. Maybe that's all you needed. Ten minutes of good material. The idea was incredibly exciting. I could come up with ten minutes. It might take a year, but I could do it. But no. Yes. No. Slowly, over the course of several months, my fantasy moved off the absolute end of the continuum—the realm of the impossible—with the gravest repercussions for my emotions and my body.

I could no longer fantasize with impunity. Now when I pictured myself on stage with a mike in my hand looking down on the expectant faces, my body believed it was happening. My heart would race, my mouth would go dry, and sometimes I would experience absolute terror. My fantasy was no longer fun, but there was an excitement about it which was heady, and it became addictive. I continued to fantasize, but not as often and only during the day. A nighttime fantasy would pump enough adrenaline into my system to keep me awake till dawn.

On November 22, 1977, I had a dream which gave a new meaning—a spiritual one—to humor. Meher Baba was sitting across a table from me. I looked at him and observed all the details of his face. He looked back into my eyes. Suddenly he began to make funny faces, one after the other. I began to giggle in the dream and then I entered a state of euphoria—a dream experience I had never had before or since. When I awoke, the dream remained vivid. I can still conjure up the images of Meher Baba's funny faces.

When I began taking classes at the Synthesis Graduate School in San Francisco, I discovered a number of comedy clubs nearby. My favorite was the Holy City Zoo on Clement Street, where Robin Williams was said to have begun his career. It had a small bar where the comics usually hung out before going on. The stage was small, too, maybe eight by eight, and about seventy-five people could squeeze into the narrow space in front of it. Cozy, intimate, dark. I would usually go on Thursdays—one of the open mike nights—and watch the aspiring comedians, young men mostly, a few women, repeating the same jokes and stories, occasionally adding, deleting, changing a line. I was always excited, sometimes laughing, other times feeling acute embarrassment when the material fell flat. I got to know some of them. They would circulate from club to club, performing six or seven nights a week, honing their material, waiting to be discovered. One of the funniest was Mike Pritchard. Another was Paula Poundstone. Years later they made appearances on the "Tonight Show."

My Comic Subpersonality Wanted to Stand Up

In my psychosynthesis training, we were learning techniques to make us aware of our subpersonalities. The students would often practice with each other—one as guide, one as client—under the supervision of a faculty member. When I was the client, the subpersonality that began to emerge, the one who wanted to be heard—who wanted to *standup*—was the Comic. After all, he argued, every Thursday night he was witnessing no-talent people getting up and making absolute fools of themselves. He could be as good as half of the comics on any given night. Ten minutes of good material was all that was needed, and a simpleton could come up with that. What was the big deal?

The big deal was Fear. In the world of imagery, Comic was about a foot tall, slight of build, wore glasses, and looked like a midget version of Woody Allen. Fear, on the other hand, was the size of a two-story house. Fear was not very articulate. All he could manage to say was *no!* But Fear had a direct line into my autonomic nervous system. To get my attention he might fire a few warning shots across the bow. Sweaty palms. Rapid heartbeat. Dry mouth. If I didn't back off whatever I was doing or thinking (usually the latter) that was upsetting him, he'd escalate to general body angst, what Harry Crews called the "icks." If Fear wanted to get really nasty, he could bring my body to its knees in seconds. He could constrict the vessels in my throat so that it was difficult to talk; he could make me nauseated to the point of vomiting. For good reason I did not want to mess with Fear.

Week after week we worked on my issue, using every therapeutic trick my guides and supervising faculty could think of. In guided imagery, I fed the Comic, making him bigger and stronger—he still looked like Woody Allen but had put on a few pounds and was about four feet tall. I talked to Fear, trying to get him to explain what exactly he was afraid of, but to no avail. Whatever it was was terrifying beyond words. The sense that I got from our many one-sided conversations was that Fear believed that if I stood up on that stage at the Holy City Zoo I would be annihilated. It would somehow trigger a personal nuclear holocaust. I tried to convince him it made absolutely no sense. No one, to my knowledge, had ever been executed for telling bad jokes. Maybe, I conceded, in the Middle Ages a few court jesters lost their heads, but this wasn't the Middle Ages. This was 1979. Some of my guides speculated that in a previous incarnation I had been one of those court jesters, and one evening they tried to regress me back to the tenth century so I could relive the experience. I did come up with a name, Warghol—he was the king—and Wimperfeld, the jester, and a scene in which Wimperfeld was brought before the king, who suspected him of bedding Queen Latcia (who in this guided daydream looked very much like Sophia Loren). As Wimperfeld was being subjected to some friendly torture—just a joke, said Warghol—he spat out this ditty: "Sticks and stones will break my bones, but not my boner." The king was not amused. He emasculated Wimperfeld on the spot, disemboweled him, and boiled first the parts and then Wimperfeld in oil.

My guides agreed that Fear had obviously remembered that experience and was therefore a bit reluctant to chance a recurrence. I wasn't convinced. I thought I had made up the whole story just to please my guides. I especially didn't like their conclusion—that to free myself of this thousand-year-old fear, my karma required me to perform as a stand-up comic. Otherwise, I'd have to come back in a future lifetime and do it then. I considered that and decided I had better be done with it, because in a hundred years there might not be anything to laugh about. And so I took the plunge: Before I left the San Francisco area in June of 1980, I would perform at the Holy City Zoo.

After a few months I was almost ready. Comic was now taller than Woody Allen and though he still looked like Woody, his body was more like Arnold Schwarzenegger's. In guided meditations he'd spent time pumping iron and running marathons. By similar methods, like demolition and shrinking meditations, I had reduced Fear to the size of a solid steel bowling ball which was shackled to my left leg, making walking difficult. I was scheduled to receive my M.A. in clinical psychology in about three weeks, and right after that we'd be driving back to Albany. It was time to put all the scraps of papers I had written funny bits on into some kind of sequence. In a week I had it memorized so thoroughly I could recite it without thinking. I was preparing myself for any trick Fear might pull, including withdrawing blood from my brain.

On the big night Judy wanted to go with me, but I said, "Not this time. This is something I have to do alone." Of course, I wasn't completely alone. Fear, the bowling ball, clung to my leg. I drove into San Francisco in the late afternoon and had one of my favorite dishes—scallops with black bean sauce—at a Chinese restaurant on Clement Street. The food stayed down! Triumph. But Fear managed to push my angst button and I took to the streets to walk it off. I tried—unsuccessfully—to convince my body not to listen to Fear. Air hunger, dry mouth, racing heart—what I call the minor symptoms had taken hold. I stopped outside the Zoo—it was 7 P.M., a full hour before the comics had to sign up, but I had come early to learn how to hold the mike so it wouldn't whistle—and told my body, "Look, you can puke, have a migraine, a seizure, I don't care. It's a lost cause. I'm going on, with or without you."

The guy who ran the Zoo was washing glasses behind the bar when I entered. I introduced myself, admitted I was a novice, but had twelve minutes of good material, and had come early to learn to use the mike. He agreed to show me, finished with the glasses, and a few minutes later I was on the tiny stage, practicing my *schtick* on the empty chairs.

"Not bad," said Bill, bartender, MC, and manager, "but you've got some weak spots." He proceeded to point them out. I spent the next forty minutes cutting the dead material, reworking the transitions. At eight o'clock comics began to wander in and put their names on the sign-up sheet. I added mine and ordered Calistoga water with a twist of lime.

"On the house," said Bill. I beamed and felt like a pro.

The Excruciating Wait

My day often goes by in a blink. I get out of bed. I get back into bed. Where did it go? I ask myself. I'd say about a year of it was stuffed between the hours of eight and nine on that June night in San Francisco in 1979. During that hour—or year—I watched about twenty comics come in the door and about fifty customers go to their seats. I reviewed the nearly forty years of my life and planned the next twenty. By the time Bill, the MC, took the stage my body was numb, my mood morose.

The MC's job is to warm up the audience, and Bill did it well. Some good jokes. Personal contact with a few of the people. The message: We're going to have a good time together. When I realized he was about to introduce one of the comics—and that comic might be me—I thought, "Oh my God, what have I done?" I forgot I had spent a year of my life—maybe all of my life—preparing for this night. I forgot I had a comic subpersonality. I was the introverted lawyer who had never risked trying a case. I looked at the door from my barstool perch and considered bolting. In five steps I could be out of this dark, smokey cave into fresh air, back to Walnut Creek, to Albany, and never look back. I could call my dream an aberrant obsession, which it clearly was, and declare myself cured. Unlike the twenty other comics who were milling about the bar or sitting in the audience, I didn't want to spend my time hanging out in clubs night after night. I didn't want to be discovered. I was doing this as a lark, to prove something. It had no value, it had no meaning. Now it was time to really stand up. To stand up for myself. I had stood up to Fear. I had reduced it to a manageable size. I *could* perform if I wanted to. Now it was time for me to stand up to the Comic and tell it: I refuse to subject myself to your will. There's absolutely no rational reason for doing this so I won't. No, no, no.

If I hadn't studied clinical psychology for the past two years, I'm sure I would have said, "Of course!" to my mind's forceful argument and flown out the door. But I had learned to watch the mind, for it, too, can play tricks. I knew how to observe the mind from a higher platform of being within my psyche. I remembered the metaphor for the mind attributed to Aristotle. Aristotle said the mind in its broadest sense was like a ship in which the crew—thoughts, whims, desires—had mutinied and placed the captain—the will—in the hold. One by one, in no particular order, each crew member would take over the wheel, steering in one direction or another, quite oblivious to destination. So now I was aware that my mind, or more specifically a particular thought process, wanted to take me in a direction toward which *I* did not want to go. I remember laughing to myself when I realized that Fear, so artfully inarticulate, was probably the one who had engineered my thoughts. When we seek to justify an action with an argument that's clearly influenced by our emotions, the process is called rationalization.

Instead of walking out I took a seat in the audience. For literally the next two hours, while comedians came and went, I sat pumping adrenaline at full spurt and suffered the minor symptoms. At about midnight, my well went dry and I sank into deep depression. I could barely move my body and my mind felt like a slug. During one of the breaks I went outside, hoping the night air would refresh me. In the alley near the Zoo some of the comics were smoking pot. I pretended I had a joint between my thumb and finger, brought it to my lips, and sucked in the smoke that would release me. The visualization failed. Through my ten-foot-thick head I heard someone say, "You'll be second in the next set." I found the face that said the words. It was Bill. I limped back to my seat.

The next fifteen minutes—in subjective time, two years—were among the blackest of my life. I could barely comprehend what was going on. I felt so sad I could have cried, but I didn't have the energy even for that. I dared not close my eyes because when I did I was flooded with images of being crucified. I forced myself to tune into the comic onstage and realized he was dying. No wonder they call it dying. The guy's material was bad and his delivery awkward. The expectant energy of the audience—You're going to make us laugh!—so necessary to sustain humor was gone. Mercifully, the comic surrendered the mike. Bill was going to introduce me and my biggest fear was that I would be unable to walk the twenty feet to the stage. Both body and mind were paralyzed.

"The next comedian," he exclaimed, "is a veteran of the Bay Area comedy clubs, and he has just returned from a series of performances in New York City and on the East Coast."

"Shit!" I cursed. "Why is he putting on someone else? I just want to get it over with."

"Let's hear it," Bill yelled, "for *David Tate.*"

The audience, wanting to laugh again, and now being assured that they would, for I was a veteran, a pro, clapped and cheered and their energy lifted my dead body, as powerfully as a resurrection, and brought me running to the stage. They were still clapping when I took the mike, and I had to wait a few seconds for them to quiet.

"Whenever I play in the Bay Area," I said in a voice purposefully tentative and soft, and in a tone somewhere between my own and Woody Allen's, "I like to get a feel for the audience. Are there any preoperational transsexual members of the Catholic clergy here tonight?"

The Sweetest Sound

Oh yes, there was laughter, and I tell you it was the sweetest, the richest, the most rewarding sound I had ever heard.

"How about Mormon transvestites with inverted nipples? And Jewish-Iranian lesbians for Ronald Reagan?"

Like Johnny Carson, whose audience will laugh even when his jokes are bad, I could do no wrong. I did about five minutes on sexual identity confusion, always a timely topic in San Francisco, and then went on to God. I hadn't found a smooth transition from sex to God so I asked the audience, "How do you go from sex to God?" They thought *that* was funny.

One of the nicest parts of the experience was that a part of me—perhaps afraid that, after all, I might be crucified—was watching me perform from the ceiling. I was not only doing it but was seeing myself through admiring, unbelieving eyes. I did this routine in which I pretend to be God's secretary. I answer the phone, "Kingdom of Heaven. No, God's not in. He's out smiting people. Yeah, some Ethiopians worshiping water spirits really pissed Him off. What can I do for you? You say you're a good Christian—gee, I haven't heard from one of you guys in a long time—and you want to know what to do if someone strikes you on the *other* cheek first?"

Now what's nice about that line is that it has a long fuse. You light it and wait. And hope that someone gets it and finds it funny. At the Zoo that night, a few people on the right side of the audience began to laugh and then the laughter spread like rows of falling dominoes across the room. Oh yeah. This was music. This was play.

"I don't know," I went on, perplexed at the question. "The Good Book says you're supposed to turn the other cheek. . . . But you say he hit you on the other cheek first. How about if you just bend down and let him kick you on the ass?"

When I finished my twelve-minute bit, I said, "God you've been a great audience." Words heartfelt and heartsent. They cheered so loud I'd swear I floated off that stage, along the bar, where I heard a voice say, "Nice gig," and out the door into a new, exciting world. I continued to float ten feet tall, marveling at the mystery of how after forty years I could discover I was not who I had appeared to be at all. How could it be? I marveled. How could I have done that? Who am I, really? Peak experience. Ecstasy. Awe. Wonder. Transcendence of self. Cosmic play. The vessels of these words filled with meaning. Then a snapshot—no words, just a picture—of beautiful Sophia Loren. And my feet touched down upon the earth.

My performance as a comic broke down barriers in my self-perception. The house I inhabited was much roomier than I had imagined it to be. If I could do that, I thought, something so alien to my nature, I could do anything. All dreams became possible. And with that realization, life became even more exciting. My performance was like a tonic that fortified my will to live.

CHAPTER 17

New Age Comic

In mid-June 1980 we disposed of our household possessions in a garage sale, said good-bye to friends, and set out in our station wagon for Albany. I felt the first bite of sadness as we drove up the street from the cul-de-sac and headed toward the freeway. How could I possibly go home? How could I leave the beauty of the Bay Area? The comedy clubs? My friends, most of whom were staying on for a third year?

Our return was purposely slow. We often camped in state and national parks. There was plenty of time to think. I had become a new person: more honest, more vulnerable, more feeling, more alive. I was aware of my fear that back in Albany this person would disappear, or, more accurately, be hidden beneath the masks and coats of armor I'd put on out of habit. With each mile we drove I experienced more regret. Judy had similar feelings. We considered turning back but decided that wasn't sensible. We would spend a year in Albany and then, if we still wanted to return to California, we would.

Judy took a high-pressured job. I gave some workshops on psychosynthesis and obtained a few clients. However, I soon realized that building a private practice in psychotherapy would not be easy. A master's degree in clinical psychology had no standing in New York. I could not even call myself a psychologist—a name reserved for those with Ph.D.'s who had passed the licensing examination. In California I would be eligible to be licensed as a Marriage, Family & Child Counselor. Then there was the weather. After escaping Albany win-

169

ters for two seasons, the prospect of spending five months of every year in the cold was depressing.

I began a novel. I started to develop an office building on a parcel of land I owned with my brother. But I felt out of sync, unable to find a natural rhythm.

Before leaving California, I had performed a few more times, once at a place called The Punch Line where I was able to bring my sons. (They had given me a mediocre review: I was better than some of the comics and worse than others.) I was surprised how much I missed doing stand-up comedy. When an Albany nightclub advertised that it would begin to have comedy nights once a week, I was there the first night and went on with a stage name, David Allen. It was November, the day Ronald Reagan was elected President. My material went over well. The favorite joke of the evening was my, "People are afraid that if Ronald Reagan is elected, he'll become senile in office. My question is: How will we know?"

I was back at the club the following week, this time with more finely honed material and a slightly bloated ego. When I arrived about nine-thirty, the MC looked morose. Four comics had gone on and the audience wasn't laughing. I had made them laugh last week. Would I go next to change the energy around? Of course, I said. No problem. I drank a glass of ginger ale and watched the comic on stage say his last lines and then disappear into the darkness.

"Our next comic has come all the way from San Francisco," the MC announced enthusiastically. I walked to the stage, feeling cocky. I would knock them dead.

I told one joke, then another. Some of the forty or so people looked up from their drinks, but no one laughed. I told the Reagan joke. Nothing. I went on to a story embedded with gags. I was competing with a buzz of voices. Intimate conversations. How could this be? I was funny! When I realized what was happening, I wanted to run from the stage. The ginger ale I had drunk was congealing into a lump of ice in my stomach. I remember thinking: This is show biz. I can't quit. I have to finish my material. And I did. Twelve excruciating minutes. Not one laugh. Not even a chuckle. When, mercifully, it was over, I sat down at the MC's table.

"Helluva way to make a living," I said, trying to be cool.

"I don't understand it," he said, shaking his head

Transformative Dying

I didn't either. But I was focusing on something else: the way I was feeling. When I was onstage it felt—literally—as if I were dying. The longer the audience ignored me the more diminished I felt. If only they had booed! The phrase "a blow to the ego" seems particularly apt. I felt initially shocked. Then stung. But then something very strange happened. I realized I was sitting down in a chair. I still felt emotionally bruised, but my limbs were still attached to my body. I was still breathing. I hadn't died after all. The relief I experienced was not as profound as I felt at the lake, but it was powerful. I felt light-spirited. The absolute worst had happened and yet there had been no serious repercussions. I left the club, acutely aware of a new sense of freedom. I could fall on my face. I could fail. Look how easy it was.

During the next few months I became increasingly dissatisfied living in Albany. When the sub-zero temperatures and the snow came, my desire to return to California became an obsession. I wrote long lists of reasons to go, the reasons to stay. In looking back, I realize the essential conflict revolved around my father. As much as I wanted to live in California, I didn't want to hurt him. Judy was content to remain, but she agreed to move—permanently, no more moves!—if that's what I really wanted. We made the decision in May 1981. That summer we flew to California and bought a house in Pleasant Hill and put our own house on the market.

"I don't understand it," my father would say to me again and again.

"I have to do it for my career," I would reply.

I felt terribly guilty. My father was eighty-three and my mother seventy-eight. I might not see them again. But I was convinced it was something I had to do.

I drove to California in August with the boys and our dog, Samantha. Judy flew out a month later when her job was finished. I enrolled in a couple of courses at JFK that I needed in order to sit for my

MFCC licensure examination. I also joined an ongoing workshop led by Charles Tart, a leader in the transpersonal movement. The workshop was designed to help us become more grounded in our own experience, in our own reality, to help us become more fully awake. The practice, which I'll describe later on, was of enormous help when I had to deal with another crisis that was still five years away.

I was working on new comic material when it occurred to me that the New Age was an obvious target. I wrote and distributed a brochure entitled, "Workshops Beyond The New Age: Coming Home to Yourself." Then I got a call from Harry Sloan. I had met Harry when he was on the faculty of the Synthesis Graduate School. He had been a dentist in Brooklyn in the sixties and then went to Esalen for a weekend. He never went home. He retrained as a psychotherapist and studied with Assagioli in Italy. He had become a well-respected group process leader and teacher. He was known for his wit—his marvelous, often zany, sense of humor. When I was preparing myself to do stand-up comedy, he had been enormously supportive and helpful. Now he needed my help. He had been asked to perform at a fund-raiser before hundreds of people. He was to be Swami Suchabanana, a character he had created. Would I be his straight man? Perhaps his "disciple"? Introduce him and then ask him questions?

Hahahanda Is Born

The night we performed Harry was nervous as we waited our turn to go on. He was still joking, throwing off one-liners, breaking me up. After my brief introduction, Harry—Swami Suchabanana—spoke in a near-perfect Indian accent, offering new and outrageous truths about the nature of reality. He was the only swami in the world to endorse a breakfast cereal—Pepy-Pepies. It didn't snap, crackle, or pop. It ommmmed. My part was very small. I asked a few questions. Harry's answers brought roars of laughter from the audience.

The word spread. We were asked to perform at a graduate school faculty meeting. This time I gave myself a bigger part and an identity. I was Hahahanda, the only disciple of Swami Suchabanana. I told the audience about the many New Age "trips" I had taken before I met my guru. Because I had taken quite a few workshops and was familiar with most of the New Age concepts, my story was credible. All I had to do was switch a word or two to get a laugh. Primal screaming, a well-known form of expressive or cathartic therapy, became for Hahahanda primal whining. Rebirthing became rediapering. I did five minutes. The laughs I received convinced me that Hahahanda should have an even larger role.

My last performance with Harry was a radio show. We did our usual routine and then talked, as therapists, about the benefits of laughing.

I continued to collect new material for Hahahanda. When I had about thirty minutes, I applied to perform at the 1984 Association for Transpersonal Psychology annual conference.

The conference of about five hundred people was held at Asilomar, the beautiful facility on the Pacific south of Monterey. I was scheduled for the time slot right after lunch. Because I would be competing with other workshops that were being given concurrently, I decided at the last minute to self-advertise. I put on my costume—sandals, long blue robe, rubber nose and glasses, and umbrella hat—and walked to the dining hall. I felt ridiculous. Show biz, I told myself. People looked at me, smiled, looked at the schedule of events. When I went on at one, there was standing room only and not much of that.

Hahahanda told the group how he had met his guru. The material was right for the audience. I was gently laughing at myself. The audience could identify with the spiritual seeker who sometimes tried too hard and who did silly things. They could laugh, too. It was fun, but it was more than that. It was healing. Foibles were acknowledged and forgiven.

Since that 1984 conference, Hahahanda has performed a number of times. The most memorable performance was at Esalen in 1985. Like many happy occurrences, it was unplanned. I had attended the 1985 ATP conference at Asilomar and Hahahanda again performed. After the conference I drove to Esalen to take a five-day screenwriting course. I had checked in and gotten settled in my cabin when one of my two roommates arrived. He was a lawyer from Los Angeles. He, too, had been at the ATP conference.

"Did you see the comic?" he asked. Because I had worn the rubber nose and glasses, he didn't recognize me.

"No," I said. I couldn't resist. "Tell me about him."

He began to pour superlatives on him—on me! "He was one of the funniest people I'd ever seen," he said, and I listened gleefully. Smiling, I pointed to my face.

"It was me." I took out my nose and glasses and put them on. He was delighted. "You have to do it here," he said. "You must. I'll arrange it."

Not only did he arrange a place, but the publicity as well. On the day of the performance strangers approached me to say an incredibly funny person was going to entertain us that evening. Don't miss it! I promised them I wouldn't.

An Unforgettable High

I geared the material to an Esalen audience. "Yeah, I was so confused I consulted an Esalen Ouija board. It shrugged." The response to Hahahanda's story was splendid. Splendiferous, if there is such a word. It produced an unforgettable high, and to make sure I wouldn't forget, someone videotaped my performance and the audience's reaction. Whenever I watch it, it's always through the eyes of a child. With complete absorption and wonderment.

Later that evening at Esalen I went to the baths. I sat in a tub of warm water and watched the beautiful sky. Falling stars. People sitting in the next tub, retelling my jokes and laughing. Heaven.

I've often reflected that Assagioli called humor a transpersonal or spiritual quality. He believed that it was both our privilege and responsibility to manifest all of the spiritual qualities—love, beauty, courage, truth, to name a few—in the world. I've been greatly influenced by his thoughts as well as by my dream of Meher Baba and the funny faces, and so I like to think of myself as attempting to be the conduit of humor into the world. This belief system presupposes that humor, and other virtues, come from a Higher Source. When we open ourselves to this Source, whether through prayer or meditation or concentration, we may be the beneficiaries of its gifts. But the gifts are not meant to stay within us, but to flow through us.

I've joked to my audiences that I'm on the Humor Path to Self-Realization, but, in reality, it's no joke. In order to perform I needed to build a strong ego, have a good sense of myself, be confident in who I am. But to perform well, I must forget myself. My ego must grow small. Deep within I must acknowledge that like the healer I'm merely a vehicle for one of God's great gifts. And so I search for gentle humor. I tell others what I have to offer. Expression in the world requires that. I prepare the best I can for the performance. And then I try my best to get out of the way. I call this a spiritual path, a spiritual discipline, because getting out of the way is, for me, not always easy and never fully successful.

CHAPTER 18

Unfinished Business

We returned to Albany in June 1982. I need to now go back to our second stay in California, our "permanent move" which lasted just nine months.

For the first couple of months Judy and I worked together on our new house. We painted rooms, put up shutters, took up the worn carpet, and put down hardwood floors. Judy began looking for employment—her specialty was working with children—and she soon found there were no positions available. Children cannot pay for psychological services and quite often neither can their parents. The reduction in funding by the Reagan administration led to a job crisis for people in her field. She even tried volunteering in several of the excellent programs affiliated with Oakland and San Francisco hospitals. Her credentials were excellent. Her offers to volunteer were at first enthusiastically received by the medical director, but the head of the psychology department inevitably turned her down. We concluded the presence of a professional volunteer would be too threatening to the psychologists who were in danger of losing their jobs because of the cutbacks. Whatever the reason, Judy's inability to find a position became a major stress in our lives.

I encountered the same problem. I didn't have my MFCC license, and even if I had, there were few opportunities for a beginning therapist. To make matters worse we suddenly found ourselves in financial difficulty. The office building I had developed in Albany was finished, but we had no tenants. I had gambled that during the six-month construction period leases would be signed. But the market had become soft. My brother and I were going deeper and deeper in debt to pay the mortgage on the building. And we foresaw that our credit with the banks would soon run dry. Then what? I didn't know. Interest rates climbed to 18 percent. Our house in Albany never sold, and we had rented it so that we could pay the expenses.

I felt responsible for all our problems. I was the one who insisted we move back to California. It had been my decision to put up the office building. I worried about our situation. I became anxious and depressed. And Judy grew frustrated and angry.

Depression Takes Hold

I remember watching the depressive process take hold of me. At first I couldn't believe it was happening. I thought of myself as emotionally stable. I understood the dynamics of anxiety and depression. I knew that a withdrawal of self-love, of self-esteem, could trigger a depression. I could see this was happening, but I felt powerless to stop it. I began to experience more severe anxiety symptoms—first constrictions of the throat, then gagging and vomiting. A part of me remained aloof and continued to watch as I experienced these symptoms. At times it seemed bemused. It seemed to know that my experience was incongruent with who I was. I was, after all, stable, secure in myself, even wise. But my body and my emotions had forgotten that. "They" thought I was falling apart.

As I entered more deeply into what I thought of as psychoneurotic process, I knew I needed help. For over a month I resisted that thought. I was a therapist. I would cure myself.

Judy's anger was expressed in superficial ways. She was impatient with me, annoyed. Our relationship became strained. But fortunately for me she had not yet experienced the deep source of her anger.

All these years I had insisted on keeping my illness a secret, and Judy had acceded to my wishes. For over a decade she had been unable to express her own feelings, to share them with a friend or even with me. For the first two years of my illness, I had been absorbed in my own world of worry and dread. Then, after the revelation, I was hell-bent on survival. How she was feeling was rarely discussed. Judy had every reason to be furious.

In my fragile state, I would have been devastated if she had lashed out at me. It was soon to come, her passionate outpouring of pain and rage, and I, with the help of a good therapist, became strong enough to receive it.

It happened like this. I received in the mail one day a postcard that stated, "Rollo May invites you to come for an evening to his home in Tiburon, Sunday, April 4, at 7:00 P.M. Dr. Laura Gilot is visiting from Rome and she will be sharing with us her new research under the title, *New Paradigms in Psychosynthesis.*" Directions were given to Rollo May's home and his telephone number was supplied to R.S.V.P. Rollo May was one of my heros. I had read his work when I was an undergraduate nearly thirty years before receiving the invitation. It seemed like a good omen. I asked Judy to join me, but she refused. I decided to go without her. I remember calling the number on the card and being astounded when Rollo May actually answered.

As I drove to Rollo May's home, I fantasized that he would become my therapist. For the first time I accepted the fact that I needed a therapist and I needed one right away. My symptoms were getting worse. The week before, I had left the house after having an argument with Judy. I was on my way to give a humor performance with Harry Sloan. When I got into my car, I began to cry and I cried for over half an hour until I arrived at my destination. I went into the building, found the men's room, and washed my face. Ten minutes later I was on the stage as Hahahanda, making people laugh.

Tonight, I was the first guest to arrive. Rollo May greeted me at the door. I knew from his writing that he was a creative thinker, a wise man. Now, in my vulnerable and sensitive state, I felt his warmth. We stood at a counter in his kitchen slicing carrots and celery, and I told him what I was going through. Would he be my therapist? Yes, he said, but he would not be able to see me for three weeks. I think he had some traveling commitments. I told him that as much as I wanted him to be my therapist, I realized I needed immediate help. We agreed that if I was not able to find another therapist, I would call him.

Our conversation in the kitchen, as brief as it was, was therapeutic. I had been able to tell a caring listener that I was in pain, I felt as if I was falling apart, and I needed help. This acknowledgment allowed me to take the next step—to find a good therapist.

I began the next day by calling a former professor and asking for a recommendation. He arranged for an appointment the following day with a former student of whom he thought highly. This therapist had developed a very dynamic cognitive approach that often proved effective in a brief course of therapy. I met with the therapist, a man about my own age, for an hour and a half. I explained what I thought were my problems: I felt terribly guilty and inadequate because I had placed my family in financial jeopardy; my wife was unhappy; I was confused; although it seemed ludicrous, I thought it might be best to return to New York. He reframed my self-accusations. He pointed out the fallacies of my self-condemnation. In a very logical way he tried to lead me to conclude that I really had no problems at all. I only thought I had problems, and if I changed my thinking about my situation, my so-called problems would dissolve. As for staying in California or returning to New York, it really made no difference. I could make either choice work out fine.

Everything the therapist said was probably true, but after leaving I didn't feel any better. I still felt anxious and depressed, fragile, incapable of making decision, a failure. The next day, after my class in family therapy was over, I went to the professor and asked if I could see him privately. I had observed Marty Kirschenbaum doing therapy with families. He seemed a master at the process. He was both powerful and gentle. When he realized how badly I was hurting, he agreed to see me right away. I saw him two to three times a week for several weeks. After my second session with Marty I sensed I would be well soon.

The timing of my turnaround couldn't have been better. I remember coming home from a particularly healing session feeling so much stronger, as if all the pieces of myself were being put back together. Judy, having finally made contact with her long-repressed anger and rage, exploded when I walked in the door. Volcano. Earthquake. Either metaphor seems apt. She lacerated me with her white-hot words and I thanked God—thanked Marty—that I was strong enough to stand there and take them. Since I had first been ill, she had blindly acquiesced in everything I wanted. The family secret, the silence I had imposed, was only the tip of the iceberg. She had submerged her will, her self, so many times because of the horrible possibility that I might die. That was over. That was finished. She would never do that again. As for the future, she wasn't sure she wanted one with me.

A Most Healing Hug

The central issue in my therapy was my unhealthy dependency. For many reasons, I was still attached by umbilical cords that stretched three thousand miles to my father, to my brother, and to my mother. In order to get well, I knew I had to sever those cords once and for all. In therapy I experienced my own rage at my dependency. At the end of one deeply cathartic session, Marty hugged me and assured me I would be all right. It was the most healing thing he could have done. I felt empowered by his strength and confidence. With one clean snip, the father-brother dependency cord was severed. Within a few days, a different cord, the one attached to my mother, was finally ruptured. My symptoms had significantly abated. I was nearly well. One other dependency cord had to be cut—the one connecting me to Judy.

I had asked her if she would go to see Marty with me so that we could talk about our marriage. She said no. Before she agreed to seek help to work on our relationship she first had to recommit herself to our marriage. She wasn't ready to do that.

I flew back to Albany for a week to explore the possibility of working in a therapy center. Judy and I had agreed, in principle, that we would move to the first place where one of us could find work. I remember the exact moment when my symptoms disappeared completely, the moment when I felt whole again. I was visiting my parents. About nine o'clock I went to the phone and called Judy in California. I asked her where we stood. She told me that she was still undecided. At that instant I made a decision, not a thought-decision, but a feeling-decision. It came to me that just as I could survive in the world without the help or support or even the love of my family, I could *survive* without the support and love of my wife. I could *survive* without her. I would not die. That realization startled me. And it freed me. It was not the way I wanted it to be. I loved her. I wanted us to continue as a couple. Life is more than survival. But if she chose otherwise, I'd survive. At that moment, the last remnants of anxiety—a constricted throat—disappeared and never returned.

When I returned to California, I'm sure Judy could see I was myself again. I had accepted the position in the therapy center in Albany. Our Albany tenants would be leaving in June and so we could return to our own house. I intended to make a major effort to lease the still-vacant office building.

Slowly, during that final month in California, we came together again. We took long walks, sometimes arguing, sometimes talking, sometimes in silence. Necessarily our relationship changed. Its atoms—discrete, subtle, unseen—had shifted like desert sands after a windstorm.

Even the Strongest Love Has Limits

Although it was not easy, I had to accept the fact that love, no matter how strong, has its limits. It is not—nor should it be, I realized—unconditional. In a contest between one's integrity—doing what's necessary for one's own essential well-being—and love for another, love must lose. This view might not be romantic, but I believe it's morally and psychologically sound.

I could no longer trust Judy to love me under all circumstances. Even if she did love me, she might choose not to share her life with me. The fearful heart rebels against such thoughts. Till death do us part, it says. But the loving heart accepts them. We should never be victimized by love.

One of the subjects that was discussed in our many talks was telling the boys about my illness. For a long time Judy had felt they should know. I had resisted telling them. I never wanted them to find out.

Nor did I want them to learn I had lied to them throughout their childhood. More than once when they saw my stomach at a beach, they would point and ask, "Daddy, what's that?" The "that" was the scar from my spleenectomy. I would reply, "That was caused by an operation to remove my appendix." Or they would notice the four tiny blue dots on my stomach and back and ask about them. "Birthmarks," I would say, though, in fact, they were tattoos I had gotten during radiation therapy in 1969, permanent markers to clearly delineate the boundaries of the courses of radiation to avoid overlapping dosages.

I agreed to tell the boys "soon," but managed to put it off for another year. Then, one Saturday morning after breakfast, Judy said, "Now's the time. You promised." I nodded. I felt terrible about what I had to do, for even though Chris was seventeen and Dave fourteen, I still wanted to protect them from the awful knowledge and any worry it might cause.

Judy called them into the kitchen and said, "Your father has something to tell you." For several moments I was unable to find the words. We sat in uncomfortable silence. Finally I blurted it out. I looked into their eyes and asked how they felt. Relieved, they both said. "I thought something terrible had happened," said Chris. "Yes," said Dave. "I thought you and Mom were going to get divorced." They left the table and went about their business.

PART IV.

———

Survivor's Debt

CHAPTER 19

Making Up for Lost Time

J ust before we were scheduled to drive across the country, my father, then eighty-four, had a major heart attack. I flew home immediately and visited him every day in the hospital. As I saw him making progress, finally moving off the critical list, I realized that one of the most important traits my father had given me, whether by example or genes, was the will to survive. Much of his early life had been a struggle for him. He came from Italy with his parents when he was a child. His father, a laborer, and his mother had both died young. He was mocked because of his Italian heritage and ridiculed because of his size. His adult height was five feet, one. His own parenting had sometimes been brutal.

When my father was about eleven or twelve, he had misbehaved in a way that really angered my grandfather. He was going to teach his son a lesson he would never forget. He arranged for a friend to meet him at the canal that ran through the town and told him his plan. At the agreed time, my grandfather dragged my father from their house and took him to the canal. There, he told him he was so angry he was going to drown him. He then threw my father into the canal and held him under. Within a few seconds, my grandfather's friend arrived and, as planned, pushed my grandfather aside and pulled my father from the water. My grandfather told him the next time he might not be so lucky. He had better not disobey him again.

A Deeply-Felt Message: Don't Disobey

I can't remember my thoughts when, as a child, I first heard that story, but right now I can picture that child sitting at our kitchen table where, except on special holidays, we took all our meals, and listening to my father, who always spoke a little too loudly, describe how his father had dragged him from their small house on Saratoga Avenue to the canal, dragged him wordlessly. And then, that brutal moment when my grandfather took my father's small trembling body and with his strong laborer's arms raised him in the air and flung him into the canal. I can see my father raise his finger and point it at my face as he tells me, "And that is what my father did to me." And I, the child, felt pity for my poor father and gratitude that he would never do such a terrible thing to his son, but also fear, for there was a message in the story, a warning in his finger, which entered my body like a chill.

I don't remember thinking about the story as a child, but surely I was reminded of it, felt its impact, whenever my father said, "You had better clean the basement . . . or else." Or when my mother would warn me, "Do your chores before your father comes home. You don't want to upset him."

And so, though the message was never intended, still it was probably felt at some deep level of my child's mind: If you disobey your father, you might get killed.

I remember being slapped on the face by my father. It didn't happen often—perhaps only a few times. But enough for me to remember the terrible insult to my soul, which was much worse than the hot sting on my face. Sometimes it was for teasing him. Once I had done nothing, but he thought that I had. From his perspective, based upon his experience as a child, I suppose the slaps were hardly any punishment at all.

My father was a fighter, and for that, I thank him. He had a sense of family and took his obligations seriously. He put himself and a younger brother through law school and a sister through nursing school. He worked hard as a lawyer and put his four children through college. Despite his chronic aches and pains, he never lost his zest, his enthusiasm, for life.

When he was out of danger, I flew back to California and we packed up the house. This time as we drove east I was eager to get home. There was much to do.

Wearing Many Hats

Upon returning to Albany in June 1982 I felt the need to live at full throttle. My first concern was finances. I needed to rent the office building, which was draining us. Judy designed a brochure and we had Chris and Dave distribute copies in neighboring office buildings. I put advertisements in the newspapers and called real-estate agents. Within three months we had three tenants and before the year was out, the building was nearly full. I had begun doing therapy in the counseling center. I enjoyed the process very much. I felt comfortable with my skills. I thought that in most cases I was helping to make lives better.

In addition to therapy, I sometimes gave workshops in psychosynthesis and autogenics. During that first year home, I also did some legal work. My area of expertise was appellate law. When attorneys asked me to handle appeals, I did it gladly.

I liked, or thought I did, wearing many hats. I took on the development of a retail building and it was very successful. Why stop? I took on other projects.

An agency advertised for a male therapist to work with juvenile sex offenders. It was part-time, only one day a week. I was interested in working with adolescents and took the job.

What about charity? I wasn't doing enough. Twenty-five dollars here, fifty dollars there. What did it amount to? Tokenism. Yet people were starving. They couldn't afford decent housing. That was intolerable. Look what Paul Newman and A. E. Hotchner had done. Started a business, Newman's Own, and donated all the profits to charity. Millions of dollars donated to charity. I wanted to do something like that. What? I didn't know. For over a year I was obsessed with doing something *significant* for charity. Then it came to me. I would develop a small retail complex and donate all my profits. I searched for the right parcel and finally found an acre for sale in a commercial area. I brought in investors to buy the land. I retained 50 percent and pledged that my share of the profits would be donated to charity. There were problems with the site, problems with financing, problems with construction, problems with leasing, but there were always problems. I would make it work. I had to make it work.

And my writing. What about that? I was, after all, a writer, a novelist. I hadn't published because I hadn't spent enough time *working* at it. I pulled from the bottom drawer a novel which had been through many drafts and which had been read by both Harry Crews and Albany novelist Bill Kennedy in 1978. Kennedy had said some nice things about it. It needed another draft, but it was salvageable. Work, more work. I wrote the next draft, which turned out to be an entirely new novel. Another Albany novelist suggested I send it to his agent. I did. A few weeks later I went to New York City to meet him. He liked my writing, he liked the novel, but it wasn't finished yet. It needed more work. More work. I was up for that. I liked work. My life was a frenzy of work.

I liked the agent from the start. He was open, warm, sensitive. He loved books. He was successful. And he liked my writing, he liked what I was trying to do. I told him about an idea I had for another novel. Do that one first, he advised. That will be much easier to sell.

And so I went home and wrote it, between and around everything else. I wrote the first draft in eleven weeks. I sent it to the agent to see what he thought. What he thought was that it was good enough to send to publishers. In fact, he thought it was so good, especially for a "first" novel, that he was going to multiple-submit it to twelve publishers and try to get an auction going. I was ecstatic. I was going to have a novel published! Nearly twenty-five years ago my first novel had been sent around by John Schaffner. Now I was going to have a novel published!

It was early July, 1986. I thought that surely by August nineteenth, my forty-fifth birthday, I would have a contract. That was my hope, my expectation, my dream.

As I looked back upon our four years since returning to Albany I thought how fortunate we were. Judy had found a rewarding position working with children. We had reconnected with old friends and made new ones. Our oldest son, Chris, had just finished his freshman year of college, and Dave was entering his senior year of high school. I no longer resented the cold winters, but instead took up skiing again. I was doing everything I wanted to do.

Novelist. Psychotherapist. Real-estate Developer. Lawyer. Stand-up Comic. Look how many hats I wear. See my hats. Aren't they beautiful?

CHAPTER 20

Two Steps
Backward: A Heart
Attack

B ecause our lives were an abundance of good things and because
we so much enjoyed parenting, Judy and I decided to adopt a
child, a girl child. We applied to a local adoption agency that sponsored Korean children and in mid-July went to the first series of pre-
adoption seminars. A second two-day seminar was to begin on Friday, August twenty-second, three days after my forty-fifth birthday.
I had some reservations about having another child. Because I took
parenting so seriously, I would have to cut back on something. I
wasn't sure what. But as I thought of having our third child, a daugh-
ter (and surely, later on, there would be a fourth!) my doubts dissolved. It felt right. It was meant to be.

My forty-fifth birthday was a work day and I was not happy about
it. I was one of several people involved in developing a shopping center. A meeting had been scheduled to negotiate a lease with a large
supermarket chain. I had planned to swim the lake where my family
had spent summers when I was a child, to celebrate my birthday and
to prove how fit I was. I was, I believed, in excellent health. Although
I didn't exercise enough—I swam on average twice a week—and my

cholesterol was a bit high, 227, I was lean, rarely ate red meat or pork, and my blood pressure was a low 90 over 60. I remember a physician friend, a psychiatrist, telling me I would never get a heart attack. I believed him. And three days before my birthday I had been checked by Dr. Siow, who was visiting New York. I was, he assured me, in balance.

I Swam After the Dog, Afraid She'd Have a Heart Attack

I spent my birthday, from nine till six, including a working lunch, negotiating the lease. On the following day my sons, Samantha, and I went to the lake. We put Sam in a rubber raft and Dave and Chris took turns paddling while the other swam. I swam about a mile and a quarter to an island at the other end of the lake without difficulty. After we rested, we all took turns in the raft on the way back to shore. Sam had plenty of time swimming at the island but apparently wanted more. In she went and with her powerful paws began paddling toward the shore about a quarter of a mile away. I jumped in and swam after her. I did the crawl as fast as I could in an effort to reach her. As crazy as this may sound, I was worried that, given her age—nine—the exertion might give her a heart attack. When I got to the bank, I was huffing, but I felt good. This *proved* I was in good shape. This proved *my* heart was strong.

The next day, the twenty-first, I had a massage from a professional masseuse, a birthday present from Judy. That evening after dinner I sat in the yellow chair in our living room and read a book written by my agent, *How to Write and Sell Your First Novel.* I thought about the fact that my novel had not sold. Twelve publishers had turned it down. It had been sent out to other publishers. But the hope, the expectation, the dream, at least for now, was gone. Yet in reading my agent's book, I started to believe again that publication was possible. The possibility was terribly exciting. Sitting in the chair that evening I experienced sadness and disappointment, but also renewed hope. I had an agent, a good agent. He believed in me. I might have to write a second, even a third draft, but eventually, I told myself, the novel would find a home.

I remember being very tired that evening. My eyes kept closing. I would rest them for fifteen or twenty minutes and then read for ten minutes and close them again. I finally went to bed.

The next morning Judy and I were at the adoption agency at nine. We listened to talks by some social workers. About eleven-thirty I began to have a stomachache in my upper abdomen. At first the pain was mild. It reminded me of the pain I had with the spastic stomach condition when I was in graduate school in 1963. The pain went from mild annoyance to severe discomfort within a half hour. I told Judy about it, and we went home. I thought that if I took some antacid and lay down I'd be all right.

I remember coming to the intersection where we had to turn left to get to our house. Judy was driving. A right turn would have brought us to Memorial Hospital, about two miles away.

"Should we go to the hospital?" Judy asked. "Just to be on the safe side?"

"No," I said. "I just need to lie down. Let's go home."

After taking antacid, I lay on our bed. I began to feel better. But then the pain got worse. I called my physician's office. She was on vacation, but her partners were there. The nurse told me to come right over. All right, I said. I assumed they would be able to give me something for my terrible stomachache.

During the fifteen-minute drive to the office, the pain began to radiate into my back. I thought I must have strained some muscles when I swam so hard at the lake. As soon as we arrived, I was hurried into a room and immediately hooked up to an EKG. "Why the EKG?" I asked. "It's my stomach." Routine, I was told. Then I saw the look of concern on the internist's face. "It's irregular," she explained. "You may be having a heart attack." I broke into a cold sweat. It had never occurred to me. At that second I went into a state of shock.

Nitroglycerin pills under my tongue. I felt as if I were going to have an orgasm. Then two walls appeared on each side of my peripheral vision. The walls started to move toward the center. My consciousness was steadily diminishing. I felt I was dying. When the walls came together, I would be gone.

I Remembered Norman Cousins's Words: Don't Panic

"I'm leaving," I announced. What I thought were my final words. Suddenly the walls stopped. I was lying on a stretcher. An oxygen tube was in my nose. Judy's face. Telling her to leave the keys so someone else could pick up the car. In the ambulance, feeling absolute terror, for I thought that at any second I might die. Overhearing someone say, "We almost lost him." The siren screaming, I thought of Norman Cousin's words, "If you're having a heart attack, the worst thing you can do is panic." Don't panic, I tried telling myself. Don't panic? How could I not panic? If I weren't so frightened, I would have laughed.

The next thing I remember was being carried into the emergency room where I was met by a cardiologist who had been called by the internist. He looked down at me and said, "You're having a myocardial infarction."

"I survived cancer twice," I told him. "I'm not going to die. Do what you have to do."

"I could give you a drug that might dissolve the clot. But it's not likely to be effective because so much time has elapsed since the onset. And there are risks. It could cause bleeding in the brain. I don't think I'll give you the drug."

I was given morphine and admitted to the intensive care unit. Whenever I awoke, Judy was there, sitting beside me. I don't remember what she said, whether she said anything. I think she held my hand.

I was in a private room. About nine that evening Judy was told by the night nurse that she would have to leave. She refused. The nurse initially made a fuss and threatened to put her out. I told her I wanted my wife to stay the night. Did she want to upset me? Endanger my condition? She backed off. Judy slept beside me in the chair.

I don't remember very much of the next few days. Chris and Dave came to see me. My brother. Several friends. Judy seemed always present. She spent the first four nights in my room.

My recovery was proceeding without complications. I knew that one of the things they were watching for was irregular heartbeat, arrhythmia. It happened just once and I remember the exact moment it occurred. I was thinking about my father. I thought, This is Thursday. He'll be expecting me for cards. He'll be angry when I don't come. It was then that my heart had a series of irregular beats. Several nurses came into the room. They watched me and the monitor closely. Within a minute my heart normalized.

On the sixth day I was moved from my private room in the intensive care unit into a semiprivate recovery room. The man in the other bed watched television all day, until the late evening. I wasn't able to rest, and that night I didn't sleep much. I was told by the nurses that nothing could be done. I told them that I could do something—I could remove myself from the hospital, and that is what I would do in the morning.

When my cardiologist arrived, I told him I couldn't rest in the hospital and I wanted to go home. He thought for a moment. Ordinarily, he'd keep me for another couple of days. But I was doing well. And it was important that I rest. He'd discharge me.

Weak, Fragile, Betrayed

I left the hospital feeling very weak, very fragile. I felt betrayed. I had fought long and hard for my health. I had had cancer. Wasn't that enough?

The heart attack made no sense. There was heart disease in my family, but my father and uncles and aunts who had it weren't stricken until their seventies or eighties. My oldest sister had had a minor attack caused by a spasm in her early fifties. But my attack, according to the CPK enzyme measure of 1940, was not minor but "moderate to severe," I was told by one of the nurses. A clot had formed in the left anterior artery. A portion of my heart muscle had died and would never function again.

I spent most days in the next few months sitting in the blue comfortable chair in the family room, looking out the window. I was told to walk, to exercise, and so every day in the first weeks Samantha and I went around the block. I usually returned very tired and often fell asleep in the chair.

Both my cardiologist and my internist thought I should have an angiogram, or catheterization, to determine the extent of atherosclerotic disease in my arteries. I would have gone along with their advice, but Robert Young questioned whether the procedure was necessary. It involved snaking a small tube from an artery in the groin into the arteries in the heart; dye was then injected into those arteries and movies were taken of the inside of the artery walls. The procedure carried risks, small to be sure—a 0.3 percent mortality. Robert flew up from Washington to speak to my cardiologist. They met at my home on a Saturday. I sat and listened, not fully comprehending their arguments. I could tell that my cardiologist resented an oncologist telling him how to treat his patient. Finally it was agreed that I would have the noninvasive thallium stress test done first. If I did well on that, my cardiologist would forgo the angiogram, at least for the present.

The thallium stress test involves running on a treadmill until you are very tired. At that point you signal the cardiologist and then a radioactive compound, thallium chloride, is injected into an IV which has already been hooked up to a vein in the arm. Three images, each lasting seven minutes, are taken of the heart. Three or four hours later the imaging part of the examination is repeated. The data are then fed into a computer. From the computer analysis and a viewing of the films, a diagnostic radiologist is able to determine if there is myocardial ischemia—a diminished blood supply to the heart—which would suggest the existence of significant atherosclerotic disease. The radiologist can also pick up significant abnormalities in the artery walls.

I was scheduled to take the test on September third, just eleven days after my heart attack. It seemed insane to have to run on a treadmill so soon after a heart attack, but Robert assured me it was routine and there were no significant risks. I had begun reading Norman Cousins's *The Healing Heart* and learned that he had taken the thallium stress test thirteen days after his heart attack. But he had been so frightened of the procedure—he knew of several incidents in which people taking the test had required emergency treatment, and in one case the person had died—that he felt faint and after a few minutes the test had to be discontinued. The results of his first test indicated that atherosclerotic blockage was present. Mr. Cousins tried retaking the test, but this time his fear of failure was so great he became woozy and the test had to be canceled. He then put himself on a regimen of exercise, stress-reducing activities, and a diet to lower his cholesterol. Six months later he went back on the treadmill but under markedly different circumstances. He devised a protocol in which he would operate the treadmill; he brought with him into the room Bach and Beethoven recordings and a Woody Allen cassette. He felt relaxed and confident. This time he spent twelve minutes on the machine. His blood pressure increased as it was supposed to. His heart responded well to the exertion.

Preparing for the Treadmill Test With Relaxation Techniques

I was determined to "pass" the treadmill test on the first try. But I had learned from Norman Cousins that I needed to be confident and relaxed. To build confidence, I repeated affirmations that I would do well; I visualized myself on the treadmill, looking relaxed. I did autogenic relaxation exercises for about an hour a day.

Judy drove me to the hospital on the day of the test. I listened to an autogenics relaxation tape made for my former mentor and now friend, Vera Fryling, in the car and in the waiting room. I experienced no discomfort during the test. I exercised for 2.5 minutes into Stage Three of the Bruce Protocol and achieved a heart rate of 135 beats per minute.

I received the report a few days later. Defects on the anterior artery were consistent with a prior myocardial infarction. There was no evidence of additional wall abnormalities or myocardial ischemia. Needless to say, I was very happy. It was possible that I had had a one-vessel incident and that I did not have general atherosclerotic disease.

In the months following my heart attack, I remained exquisitely fragile. I was content to do nothing but look out the window. I stopped doing therapy both privately and at the agency, and I disengaged from my real-estate activities, except for the plaza I was developing for charity. I no longer went each Thursday evening to have dinner and then play cards with my parents. I rarely read. I was no longer proud of having worn all those hats. Now I felt stupid. I had pushed myself too much. Now I would take off all my hats and do absolutely nothing.

The truth is, I had very little energy to do much more than exercise, which I did four to five times a week. In order to get well I knew I had to exercise. I had to change my diet. I had to meditate. I didn't know what else.

I knew that being fearful would not help my healing, and yet I was very fearful that at any moment I would have another attack. I thought I might die while walking the dog. Or in bed. I was sensitive to every twinge in my stomach or chest. My heart attack had come on so slowly, so insidiously, disguising itself as a stomachache. It was all so mysterious. Why? I wondered. Why? I asked my cardiologist. "If I knew," he said, "I'd get the Nobel Prize."

For a while I recorded all my symptoms so I could accurately report them to my physicians: "9/5, 6 P.M., intermittent pain in my right shoulder, tired, depressed; 10 A.M. had walked .7 mile and after had ache in both ears and neck—from the cold? 9/11, had occasional sharp pains in the heart; 11 A.M., sharp pain, right shoulder; 11:30, migraine aura; 6:30, pain under left shoulder; 9/14, ache in upper right side of my chest, again at 4:30; 7 P.M. pain down my right arm, brief, and later, pain in my upper right shoulder, pain in toes occasionally; 9/16, awoke with sharp pain in heart; later, 7 A.M., some pain in left shoulder, radiated four inches down my arm. Lasted five seconds. Angina?"

I really didn't know what angina felt like, whether I had ever had it. In the pamphlet "Heart Care After Heart Attack," given to me when I left the hospital, I had read that angina, congestive heart failure, and rhythm disturbances or irregular heartbeats are three potential problems following a heart attack. Angina, a partial blockage of a coronary artery, results in discomfort or pain in the chest, shoulders, arms, or neck. It typically comes during physical exertion or stress, extreme temperatures, at high alititudes, or after a heavy meal. It's often a pressing, tight feeling in the middle of the chest, varies from mild to severe, and may spread to the neck, jaw, shoulders, or arms.

When I reported my symptoms to the cardiologist, he would say, "No, that doesn't sound like angina."

If I did experience angina, I was to take nitroglycerin under the tongue in the form of Nitrolingual spray. Because I had low blood pressure, I was afraid that the nitroglycerin, which expands the arteries and decreases blood pressure, would cause me to lose consciousness. My cardiologist said he would administer the nitro in his office to prove to me this would not happen. When I went, he took my blood pressure and decided against the experiment. Instead he advised me not to take the nitroglycerin if I had angina. Rather, I should immediately go to the nearest emergency room. My internist said I should take it, but advised that I lie down first. That way if I did pass out and fall, I wouldn't hit my head.

And why was I so tired all the time? Why did I have no energy? My doctor assured me it was not my heart. My heart was performing well. Maybe it was the 100 milligrams of Tenormin, a beta blocker, that I was taking. Beta blockers decrease the workload of the heart, lowering heart rate and resistance; they also control irregular heart rhythm. I was also taking a calcium blocker, a drug that relaxes and widens blood vessels, increasing the blood flow to the heart. My cardiologist said I needed these medications. They reduced the risk of another attack. But *if*, he emphasized, I were to have the angiogram and my arteries were found to be relatively clear—and only the angiogram could absolutely establish that—I might be able to reduce the medications or even eliminate them.

I reconsidered having the angiogram. I knew of one man who died during the procedure and I had heard of other complications, including the induction of a heart attack. I had survived against much worse odds, but now I felt my luck had run out. God, fate, my own body had turned against me. No, I wouldn't do it unless it proved absolutely necessary.

A few weeks after my heart attack, Peter Herbert, a high school friend who had gone to Yale Medical School with Robert, came to see me. Peter was the friend who had visited me a few days after I had my spleenectomy in 1969 at Yale–New Haven Hospital. During my hallucination, which had been induced by the painkiller, Talwin, one of the strange things I saw was a small sapling grow into a large tree. The tree aged and withered, its top finally evolving into a human head, the head of Peter Herbert. And then Peter aged, too, his face wrinkled and cracked, and he became a Chinese man who looked to be a thousand years old.

Peter had spent his medical career studying lipids—including cholesterol. A clinician and researcher, he was head of the nutrition and metabolism department of Brown University's Miriam Hospital. He spent several hours with Judy and me, telling us about the relationship between cholesterol and heart disease. He offered to monitor my cholesterol levels.

Peter's visit remains memorable because he was so sympathetic, so kind and reassuring. Because of his clinical work with so many heart attack victims over the years, he knew their psychology. He told us that it usually took people over two years before they got over the trauma. It was natural to be frightened and even demoralized. It was nothing to be ashamed of.

Peter explained that for six to eight weeks following a heart attack it was impossible to get a reliable cholesterol reading. He said he would send me vials into which my blood could be drawn and then mailed to his lab. In order to get accurate and consistent readings, he thought it important that his technicians do the actual analysis. About two weeks before the blood test, which I was to take the first week in November, I was to go on a strict nondairy, vegetarian diet. The diet was part of the information packet he gave us. Naturally, I went on the diet right away.

The first results were very promising. About eighteen months before my heart attack, my cholesterol had been 227; it was now

175. Peter wrote a congratulatory letter. "I don't think I've ever seen this response before, but I had no reason to believe you'd conform to anybody's expectations. You realize that you're already in a low-risk category, but there's no reason not to try to transform you into a Third World Indian."

Peter recommended that I take a prescription drug, Questran (cholestyramine), to further lower my cholesterol. Before beginning the Questran, I took another blood test. My cholesterol had risen to 210. After three weeks on the Questran, it was back down to 174. The side effects, especially during the first few months on the drug, were often unpleasant: bloating of the stomach, gas, indigestion, heartburn. Initially the latter symptoms would trigger anxiety. My body would seem to stop, waiting, listening: Is it just indigestion? Is it the Questran? After taking antacid, the symptoms would abate within fifteen minutes. Then I could begin to relax.

My cardiologist told me I was silly to take the Questran. In his opinion it was overkill, completely unnecessary. He was still pushing me to have the angiogram, so I decided to get a second opinion.

Peter arranged for a consultation with a cardiologist at Massachusetts General Hospital, Dr. Andrew Bodnar. Dr. Bodnar first wanted me to repeat the thallium stress test; this was done in Albany in early January 1987. Except for the residual scar from the original heart attack, there were no abnormalities. This time I achieved a heart rate of 162, which was more than 85 percent of the maximum predicted heart rate for someone my age.

The Doctor Is the Treatment

I obtained my medical records from the hospital and from my cardiologist, and Judy and I went to Boston on a Friday. Dr. Bodnar, a pleasant, soft-spoken man about my own age—he was also a lawyer!—read the records and gave me a clinical examination as well as an EKG. He then spent nearly an hour talking with us. When I think of him, I remember Robert's words, "Sometimes the doctor is the treatment." Dr. Bodnar's soothing words of reassurance made me feel so much better. I was doing well, he said. There was no evidence of cardiac insufficiency. It was quite possible that a single lesion had formed in my anterior artery and that plaque had accumulated at that point. The lesion may have been caused by the radiation therapy I had received twenty years before the heart attack. My prognosis was good. An angiogram was not indicated, because, in his view, a patient should have the procedure only when there is a reason to believe that a surgical intervention, such as angioplasty or bypass surgery, is necessary. I had no angina, no sign of blockage or even narrowing. I was not in that category.

After the consultation, I thought it might be possible to lead a normal life again. But a part of me, the frightened child who was so identified with my body, continued to be traumatized by so close an encounter with death. Despite my experience with having cancer—or perhaps because of it—I didn't seem to have the means within me to contain this new experience. The aftereffects of the trauma continued to reverberate. At times my fatigue got so bad my mind became muddled. I had difficulty sleeping. A part of me seemed always on alert, constantly watching. I was apathetic and listless and had little interest in doing anything.

When I think of myself then, I see the image of an antique vase. Although it had been shattered, it was still apiece. Something needed to happen so that its parts would meld together again. I didn't know what it was. I didn't know what to do.

CHAPTER 21

Learning Patience

N ot knowing what to do, I did nothing. I often felt as if I were
an invalid, an old man. The physical weakness, the lethargy,
was debilitating. The deep fatigue often made me anxious at bedtime.
I would have to rest, to relax, in order to get to sleep.

When I left the hospital, I had been given Valium and Halcyon,
tranquilizers to help me sleep. Often, after four or five hours of deep
sleep, I'd awaken and be alert. I'd lie awake until morning. Some
time later I read that this was not an uncommon reaction to Halcyon.
When I discontinued using it, I slept better and felt a bit more rested
during the day.

My internist, Roberta Flesh, a close friend, was very supportive. I
sometimes called her to describe a particular sensation in my stomach
or chest. She would listen and then reassure me. No, that was not
angina. The symptom had nothing to do with my heart.

Roberta suggested that I consider getting off the beta blocker. She
believed that my tiredness and apathy were probably side effects of
that drug. I knew the drug could produce those symptoms and others. A friend of mine had been placed on the drug for high blood pressure. He became depressed, often found himself crying, and was
impotent. His doctor had not warned him that the drug might cause
these side effects. As a result, Tom, feeling he was having a nervous
breakdown, tried to hide his symptoms. When he finally went to his
doctor, he was taken off the drug.

Dr. Bodnar had said that I could safely decrease my dose of Tenormin to 50 milligrams a day. I decided I would try the reduction to

see if I'd feel better. After a week I began to notice improvement. I had more energy. I felt less lethargic. But I was still a long way from how I in felt in pre–heart attack days. I still felt like a zombie much of the time.

I spoke with Peter, my cholesterol advisor, about getting off Tenormin entirely. He told me that those who took a beta blocker were less likely to have a second heart attack than those who didn't, but the statistical advantage for those who took the drug was slight. I might not need the drug, but it was impossible to say. What would he do in my position? He thought for a minute. He would stay on the 50 milligrams if he could. But if the fatigue or other side effects significantly interfered with his ability to work, he'd get off it.

Roberta emphasized quality of life. If the drug affected the quality of my life, was the statistical edge worth it? Probably not, I thought. I waited another month, hoping my condition would improve. I didn't want to go off the drug. I wanted every advantage I could get. I went to see another cardiologist in Albany, Dr. David Putnam. After reviewing my history and giving me a physical examination, he said he felt comfortable with my eliminating beta blockers entirely. Aspirin was the only medication I really needed. It wouldn't hurt to continue with Calan—the calcium blocker. That medication was unlikely to cause side effects. He would leave the decision to me.

I liked Dr. Putnam's patient-centered approach. He did not think I was foolish taking Questran to keep my cholesterol below 180. He was bright, attentive, easy-going. I told him I wanted him to continue as my cardiologist.

Once I had been off the Tenormin for about ten days I felt much better. Still not my old self, but better. I kept my days very simple. I knew that besides controlling my cholesterol and taking aspirin I needed to exercise.

The Benefit of a Cardiac Rehab Program

I mentioned earlier that right after my heart attack I was fearful when I walked by myself. In order to overcome my fear of exercise I had enrolled in the cardiac rehabilitation program at St. Peter's Hospital. Judy came with me the first day, September twelfth. How frightened I was! I was introduced to the four machines I would be using: a treadmill, a stationary bicycle, a rowing machine, and an arm ergometer, a gadget with two handles on each side of a wheel which you turned round and round with your hands. I was told about the importance of warming up before exercising and taught warm-up techniques. Cooling down was equally important. A physical therapist designed my program. Then I was hooked up to an EKG by one of the registered nurses who were always in the exercise room, watching the monitors. I exercised just twenty minutes that first day—slowly, moderately—but for me, it was like breaking the four-minute mile. A barrier had fallen. My body, my frightened-child body, learned what my mind already knew: Exercise wouldn't kill me.

I can't say enough about the benefit I derived from the cardiac rehab program. I went three days a week for ten weeks. Each time I went I seemed able to do a little more. And the change was measurable. My entry Met level was 3.6. (Met stands for the Metabolic Cost of Activities and is a general measure of stamina and cardiac fitness.) According to the activity guidelines handout I was given, this meant I could probably do a number of things safely. Activities in the 2 to 3 Met range included: walking level at two miles per hour, cycling level at five miles per hour, bowling, cooking, lifting weights up to ten pounds, riding a power mower, and sexual intercourse.

After five weeks in the program, I was at the 5 Met level. This meant I could, among other things, paint, iron, change a tire, milk a cow by hand, lift up to thirty pounds, play golf and social doubles tennis, dance the foxtrot and waltz, and have vigorous sexual intercourse.

When I completed the program I was at 8 Mets. Now I could do pick and shovel work, lay railroad track, carry sixty pounds, shovel medium snow, do vigorous downhill skiing, engage in social racquetball, play half-court basketball and ice hockey, and perform most coal mining jobs. When I first read through the list of approved activities, I looked again for the mention of sexual intercourse. What came after vigorous sexual intercourse? That was left to my imagination.

Before leaving the program I bought a treadmill, an exercise bike, and a rowing machine and installed them in my basement. I also bought a heart watch that gave me a continual readout of my pulse while exercising. The watch allowed me to make sure that my heart-beat was in the target zone of 124 to 150, which was 70 percent to 85 percent of the maximum attainable heart rate of 176 for my age, forty-five. From what I had read, I needed to spend at least twenty minutes in the target zone if the exercise was to have cardiovascular benefit. I usually spent thirty to forty minutes in the target zone three to five times a week.

I should mention that, like most people I know, I really don't like to exercise. To add an element of enjoyment to the process I often listen to classical music. When I feel sluggish or particularly resistant, I play the marches of John Philip Sousa. I nearly always have the desire to shorten the exercise period from forty to thirty minutes, from thirty to twenty. I ask myself: Are you tired or merely bored? Invariably it's the latter. Then I give myself a mild lecture. So you're bored? I say. Millions of athletes spend hours each day training to excel in a sport. Probably another few million run twenty, thirty miles each week just for the hell of it. You're exercising because, in part, your life depends on it. And you want to quit because you're bored? Or because it feels a little uncomfortable? Are you mad? Are you insane? The lecture always works.

Reversing Coronary Artery Disease

I recently changed my exercise protocol, raising the minimum period to forty-five minutes, four times a week. The reason was an article I read in the January/February 1989 issue of *Psychology Today*. The article, one of a series in a special section on the heart, was entitled "Heart Disease in Retreat." It described the work of a San Francisco physician, Dean Ornish, who had demonstrated experimentally that coronary heart disease could be reversed. Up until this time, as far as I was aware, there had been only anecdotal evidence of such reversal—individual cases—and no scientific studies which clinically proved that any interventions could reverse atherosclerotic process.

The "Optimal Lifestyle Program," codirected by Dr. Ornish and researchers Larry Scherwitz and Shirley Brown, had three elements: a strict low-fat, low-cholesterol diet; three hours of aerobic exercise each week; and one and a half hours of daily stress-management exercises adapted from yoga.

As soon as I put down the article I picked up the phone and called the University of California at San Francisco. Larry Scherwitz was available and, bless him, he spoke to me for about half an hour. I first wanted to know how they measured their results. The article had stated that ten of the twelve patients in the experimental group on the optimal lifestyle program showed an average overall reversal of their coronary atherosclerosis on the most sophisticated measures. What did that mean? I asked Larry. Do you do before and after angiograms on your subjects? Yes, he said. How do you justify subjecting them to that risk? I asked. These were patients who had been ordered to have catheterizations, he said. A year after they began the program, the angiograms were repeated and decreases in the narrowing of artery walls were found. A year! I marveled. Just a year!

In contrast, heart disease in the control group—those patients who followed the advice most cardiologists provide—progressed. Eleven of the seventeen people in this group got measurably worse. Of the six who got better, four were women. The two men admitted they had made some of Ornish's lifestyle changes on their own.

Larry told me that of all of the interventions he thought the stress-reduction techniques were the most important. In answer to my question, he said participants learned hatha yoga. He felt that the spiritual dimension of that discipline had special value.

After I hung up the phone, I decided to tighten up my diet. Although I am thin and have difficulty keeping on weight, I could manage with less fat intake. The increase to three hours a week of exercise would be relatively easy. An hour and a half of stress reduction exercises a day seemed a lot. But all right. I would begin with an hour and work up to it. That evening I reviewed the instructions in my yoga notebook on asanas, or hatha yoga postures, and began the practice. While in meditation, I envisioned myself to be so tiny I could stand up inside my arteries. There was plenty of room for the blood to flow past me. I took my time, gently brushing the inside of my arteries with a toothbrush. Although my arteries—the ones I saw, at least—did not appear significantly narrowed by plaque, I did see a yellowish mineral-like material here and there on the artery walls. In my imagery I am slowly scraping it away.

Sex After a Heart Attack

When I left St. Peter's Hospital after the heart attack, I was given a pamphlet which discussed issues that would be of concern to heart patients. I was amused with the way sex was handled by this Catholic institution. I was assured that if I could walk up two flights of stairs without difficulty—pain or shortness of breath—I could have intercourse with my wife. It was true, the anonymous pamphleteer pointed out, that the press sometimes reported cases of men "dying in the saddle." But in all such cases, the man, often a famous one, was having illicit sex with a younger woman. The message: It was all right to have sex, but only with your spouse.

At the cardiac rehab program I picked up a number of brochures about heart disease, one entitled "Having Sex After a Heart Attack." It emphasized that having sex was not only safe; it can be good exercise and can add to a person's sense of well-being. As for the myth that sex can be a dangerous strain on the heart: "We have probably all heard about famous men dying during sexual intercourse. But it is most important to remember that their sudden death took place—as an exciting love affair with a young girlfriend and after heavy eating and heavy drinking."

Decisions, decisions, always decisions. It seemed, at least according to this more liberal interpretation of the sex-death data, that I could survive an exciting love affair with a young girlfriend if I were willing to forgo heavy eating and drinking prior to sex. On the other hand, it seemed I'd be perfectly safe if I gorged myself with fine food, got drunk, and then had sex with a girlfriend not so young. All sorts of interesting permutations here.

I have an acquaintance who had a triple bypass operation fifteen years ago. On his first night home from the hospital he told his wife he wanted to make love. She was reluctant. Hey, he said, if we can't, why the hell did I have the operation?

I was slightly nervous the time my wife and I resumed making love. Once again the dichotomy I've suggested came into play: My mind knew it was perfectly safe; my body was not so sure. Fortunately it was easily convinced.

I did not stop the beta blockers until six months after my heart attack. During that time, as I've already noted, I spent most of my time sitting in the blue chair. Occasionally I made a business telephone call. My business partners had agreed to take over my responsibilities. My therapy clients, with one exception, found other therapists. The exception was a young woman whom I had seen for nearly three years. We needed to have a proper termination. About a year after my heart attack, when I began to have more energy on a regular basis, I saw her weekly for about six months. Our work together came to a natural end.

The Importance of Simply Being

During all those months I merely sat, I knew I had to be patient with myself. I had to give up *doing* and be content with simply *being*. It wasn't easy because part of me then—and now—wanted/wants to be productive. *I do, therefore I am.* But being, I learned from necessity, precedes doing. It is more essential, more primary. I am not talking about the metaphysical concept, *being*, but about a state of mind that not only accepts a hiatus in activity but embraces it, *values* it.

This lesson did not come easy. Even in my chair I tried to be "productive." Why had I gotten the heart attack? I had overextended myself. Too many irons in the fire. Or maybe it was the disappointment that came when I realized my novel would not be snatched up. That must have had something to do with it. The radiation therapy. That was surely the primary culprit. Peter had sent me seven article from the medical literature that reported suspicious associations between radiation treatment that penetrated the heart and coronary artery disease. I had called both Dr. Fischer and my oncologist at Albany Medical Center to see if they knew anything about the relationship between radiation and heart disease. Dr. Fischer said there was no evidence that the patients at Yale were more prone to heart disease. My oncologist reported that a study conducted at Albany Medical Center showed that pigs fed a high-fat diet and then radiated were much more likely to have coronary artery disease than radiated pigs fed a low-fat diet. All those pizzas. All those grilled-cheese sandwiches. I was one of those damn pigs!

Relax. Let it go. What difference does it make? Look out the window. The white birch in our yard. See how its thin branches dip and bow. A light wind is touching them. The pine tree across the street. Look how full it is. How green its needles. How bright! The brick walk that leads from our front door to the driveway. Judy laid it brick by brick with her hands. And Harry Crews had helped. I had forgotten that. When he visited us in the summer of 1978, he had helped her build the walk. Look. Here comes the man from down the street who had a heart attack after I did. Six months before his attack his wife had died. And then his dog, a boxer. Now he walks alone. Twice a day. Rain, snow, it doesn't matter. He, too, must want to live. Sit. Rest. Stop trying to figure out what happened. Or what you must do to take care of yourself. You know already. Exercise. Diet. And being still. When your forward momentum stops, when you are comfortable just being, you can decide what things you wish to do. But for now watch the children as they climb from the school bus. Watch the dog sniff the smell prints from our mailbox.

Watch. Be content to watch.

In my watching mode, I was reminded of what I had learned in the seminar with Charles Tart that I had taken when we had lived in California. We were instructed to become aware of our physical sensations and then of what we were seeing and hearing upon awakening. We were told to go through the day trying to maintain that awareness. Sense, look, and listen. No matter what we were doing or thinking, a part of us should continue to be aware of feelings, sights, and sounds.

I remembered that I had found the task impossible. My mind would wander and I would forget the assignment. Two or three hours later I would remember and try again. My sensory awareness would last a few minutes before I would lose it as I reentered the world of thought.

Now that I was willing to stop *doing*—planning, rehearsing, reviewing—I could simply be. Sense, look, and listen. Practicing this simple formula periodically released me from those chains of endless thoughts and allowed me to be more present in my body and in the world.

CHAPTER 22

Raking the Coals of Memory

I did not think I would have much to say about my heart attack. A part of me disbelieves it ever happened. Another part seems ever conscious of its reality. The ashes of its history are not yet cold. How could they be? At this writing it's been just two and a half years, not nearly enough time for me to assimilate the experience. In looking back, I have the image of myself raking through those still-warm coals. I see a spark, a burning cinder. That looks interesting. What's it about? Let me examine it.

Peter Hurkos. When I was a boy, I would watch the Dutch psychic on television. His eyes would be covered: layers of dough, lead, cloth. He couldn't possibly see. And yet someone from the audience would produce a dollar bill, and Peter Hurkos would accurately read the serial number.

One of my brother's friends employed Hurkos as a business consultant. Hurkos would make predictions as well as read the minds of businessmen on the other side of the negotiating table. On one of his trips to Albany in 1982 or 1983, Frank arranged for me to meet Peter Hurkos. When I was introduced, Hurkos did not extend his hand. He did not say, "Pleased to meet you." Nothing of the sort. Rather, he placed his large hand over his heart, looked deeply into

my eyes, and gasped, "The muscle! The muscle!" I was too startled
to say a word.

Varied Responses to My Heart Attack

The range of people's responses to my heart attack was not startling,
but certainly curious. I had two friends in the area whom I had
known twenty years or more who never came to see me. One of
them telephoned just once to ask how I was doing. About a year after
my heart attack he called to ask a favor. He was buying a new house.
Would I represent him? I said I would. When we met in the lobby
of the office building where the closing was to take place, I told him
I had felt badly that he hadn't reached out to me after the attack. And
I was curious why he hadn't. "I was afraid," he said. "We're the same
age. It was hard for me to deal with." Ironically, about a year later
he had a heart attack. I called him when he got home from the hospital. He seemed more eager to talk.

My other friend also telephoned just once—not so much to see
how I was doing or to express his sympathy, but to ask me what steps
he should take to avoid heart disease. Obviously, he too was afraid.
I could understand that, and yet in both instances I was disappointed
and hurt.

About three years before my heart attack I had formed a discussion
group, seven men, all therapists in their forties. Although I have no
recollection of their visits, Judy tells me each of them came to see me
in the hospital. Some of my business associates visited me when I got
home. I was particularly touched by the visit of a couple I had just
met. Natalie was a friend of Judy's and she and Eric had been our
guests at a summer party. About a week after I was home, they called
to see if it would be all right to come over the following Sunday.
Their call seemed so European—formal but warm (Eric had been
raised in Austria). We had a pleasant conversation. They stayed just
the right amount of time.

Judy's parents visited me in the hospital and were very supportive,
very concerned. My brother was there daily. My parents had been

told I was hospitalized for chest pain but were not told I had suffered a heart attack. I think the plan was that when I felt well enough, I would go see them and tell them myself. About two weeks after I was home, I felt strong enough to take the half-hour ride to their home for a brief visit. We told my father we'd be coming up on a Saturday, but when the day arrived, I was too tired to travel. Judy called to explain we wouldn't be coming. The next thing I heard was Judy screaming at my father.

"David is not well! He's recovering from a heart attack!"

Apparently my father, disappointed that we weren't coming, had started to berate her. After she hung up, Judy was shaken. She cried and I held her. My father called back and said he was driving down to see me. I told him I was going to take a nap, that now was not a good time to come. But he came anyway because, I believe, he was worried about me and wanted to see for himself that I was all right. When he arrived he apologized for yelling and seemed genuinely sad that I was ill.

A few months after the attack, an acquaintance, a prominent Albany physician I'd known for twenty years, telephoned. He hadn't heard about my heart attack and was calling to invite us to a social event. When I told him that I had had a heart attack, he said—I will never forget his words, and the unempathetic way he said them—"Oh? How did it feel?" I was flabbergasted. And hurt. How did it feel? How did *it* feel? "Not very well," I managed to mumble. I had always suspected this man was a callous fool, a self-centered twit. His inhumane response confirmed it.

But then, thank God, there are people like Robert, who as I've described flew up from Washington the first weekend I was home. And my friend Leo, who I had met in Spain in 1968. Since that time we had corresponded regularly. Every few years one of us would get on a plane to visit the other. We were the closest of friends, but still, when I called to tell him about the heart attack, I was surprised to hear him say he would come to see me. When was the best time? In a few weeks, when I'm stronger, I said. And even though his wife was about to enter the hospital for a surgery, he came. He stayed just three days, but his visit and the love it expressed meant more to me than I can say.

Expressions of Concern

I wish to emphasize as strongly as I can that when someone is seriously ill, he needs to have his friends and acquaintances express their concern in whatever ways are authentic. The words are not important. It's the feelings in back of them that matter.

My long, tortured letter to Norman Cousins. I recall it with some embarrassment—for I poured out my soul to a stranger—but also with compassion for the suffering human being I then was. I had read *Anatomy of an Illness* when it was first published. And I had once gone to Boston to hear Norman Cousins speak. *The Healing Heart*, which I carefully read my first week home, did what it was designed to do. It gave hope. I remember telephoning one of the physicians he wrote about in his book, Dr. Kleeman, because I wanted to learn more about his post-cardiac program. I had expected to speak with his secretary or nurse, and I was surprised when the doctor himself got on the phone and spoke with me for fifteen minutes.

My letter to Norman Cousins took—no exaggeration—three weeks to write. I wrote a little each day until I felt too tired to continue. I told him my life story, all I had gone through, first with the Hodgkin's and now this latest assault, a heart attack. Since he had also suffered a severe illness before his heart attack, I felt an enormous affinity with him. And because he had met both his illnesses with courage and creativity and had *survived*, I wanted him to know who I was and what I was going through. I didn't think it then, but I realize now that I wanted him to symbolically take me in and hold me, if only for an instant, in his mind and heart. I wanted him to transmit to me in a personal way some of his magnificent power.

And he did. Bless him, he did exactly what I needed him to do. He read my letter. That in itself was enormously generous, since the letter was eight pages, single-spaced. And he wrote a compassionate and encouraging reply.

Norman Cousins's letter helped to accelerate the healing process. Before I wrote my letter to him, I felt shattered. Because of the depression caused by the attack itself and compounded by the beta blockers, my struggle then, as I felt it to be, was to hold my body and soul together. Survival, plain and simple. The idea that I would ever do anything again, ever accomplish anything, was beyond my imagination, for my imagination was weighted down by my tired body and my depressed emotions. Until Norman Cousins reminded me: This is temporary; this, too, shall pass. "I have no doubt that you will find much to accomplish yet," he had written. I had no plans. No ambitions. *Accomplishment* seemed like an awfully big word. But if I stayed around—and I would do everything in my power to see that I did—who knows what might happen?

I had closed my letter to Norman Cousins with the following: "Simply writing this letter has been very helpful to me, although as I pause and reflect, I realize as much as I've tried to be honest and open, it's rather superficial. What I mean to say is there are a lot of underlying issues raised by the writing I must deal with, e.g., do I really want to go on living and why? (Pat answers won't do.) I realize, too, that simply having to ask that question suggests I am depressed, and so a few minutes ago I called an acquaintance, a psychiatrist with some very deep spiritual values, and made an appointment to see him professionally."

The person I called was Carl Mindel. He had the reputation of being one of the best psychiatrists in Albany. This time entering therapy I did not have the resistance I had in California. I knew I couldn't afford to continue to be depressed; if it continued for too long a period, it was likely to be dangerous to my overall health.

In the more than two years of therapy with Carl, we have covered a great deal of territory, much of it outside the boundaries of what I want to focus on here. I said before that I had difficulty containing the trauma of the heart attack. By that I mean I seemed unable to bear it, to carry it. A part of me was hypervigilant, always on red-alert, waiting for the next symptom to analyze and respond to. As we delved into this issue, I found that the frightened child part I've described before felt abandoned. He had no one, he felt, to rely upon, no one to help absorb his pain, no one to assure him that he would be taken care of. Therefore he had to do it all himself. The burden was too heavy. It was more than he could hold.

I recalled periods from early childhood. I was a "big boy" at five and could do everything myself. It was bad, I knew, to upset my parents. I had to protect them from worry, especially from worrying about me. Why this interpersonal dynamic between myself and my parents formed I really can't say, but I can guess. I was given messages, early on, that that's how a good boy, a big boy, behaves. A big boy takes care of his mommy and daddy.

With this developmental history I did not experience the power or strength of my father or my mother to take care of me, particularly when I was ill. As a child I was not given the calm and steady reassurance when I was sick that I would be okay. The result was that I became overconcerned with my physical well-being. My brother interpreted this concern for my body as a weakness. "You're a hypochondriac," he would often say.

In matters of personality, the inner often mirrors the outer. Our many psychological parts or subselves are often introjections of parental patterns of behavior. And so, intrapsychically, a part of me was formed from the hard crust of father-brother. This part said, "Don't you *dare* complain about being sick. Don't be afraid. Don't be a coward. You're disgusting if you do that. I won't even listen to you." Another part, this one an introjection from my mother, said, "Don't get sick. Worry about your health! If you get sick, you could die!" This had been my mother's experience. When she was fifteen, she had had pneumonia and was so close to death she had been given the last rights of the Catholic church.

Comforting the Child Within

As a result of these two components in my personality, my response to sickness or even simple symptoms was twofold. One part of me panicked. This could be life or death. I had to do something. And—I knew from those early messages—I had to do it alone. Often what I did was simply focus on the problem. This focusing, sometimes escalating to an obsession, was my way of trying to soothe that abandoned, frightened child part. And who was abandoning that frightened child? Historically, perhaps my parents, but that was no longer important. The important piece was that their introjection, now a part of me, was the abandoner. I condemned the child for whining, for being such a wimp. The result was that the child's fears would go unexpressed. They would be repressed into the unconscious where they would stir about. Then, when they saw their chance, when they perceived any tiny reason to suggest that something in my body was amiss, they would jump up screaming. They would yell *Fire!* They would cry *Wolf!* My body would respond. Tension. Anxiety. And the tough-minded punitive part would retaliate. "Shame," it would say. "You're repulsive. Hide. Get out of my sight."

One of my tasks in therapy was to understand the dynamics of these dysfunctional parts within me, the punitive abandoner and the frightened child. Then I needed to withdraw my identification from the aggressive part. This was not accomplished easily, because we have a natural tendency to identify with an aggressor, a figure that appears strong and powerful. And from a child's view, my father and brother *were* strong and powerful. Toning down the harsh, critical voice within me took time.

The child part needed desperately to be listened to and soothed. As it became okay to speak from this part, I could begin to express his fears openly; these fears no longer had to be repressed or submerged to suddenly emerge whenever a symptom could be found.

And most important, the adult part of me who was nurturing, who was a primary source of my being a good parent and therapist, had to be given a larger intrapsychic role. This part, wise and caring, tender and supportive, needed to soothe the frightened child, to let it know that it was okay to be afraid. No matter how scared it felt, it would not be left alone. *It* didn't have to worry about the body or about symptoms. The adult, the wise and powerful adult, would do those things. If I had a symptom, I, from the nurturing adult place, would decide if it might be serious. If it was, I would call Roberta, my physician, right away and ask her about it. Then I would let her decide what to do. I would let her share the responsibility for my wellness.

As a result of this phase of my therapy, I became more able to cope with symptoms, even ones that were potentially significant. I, as the more expansive, nurturing adult, could contain the trauma of my heart attack and its aftermath. The process of change was slow, because the dysfunction was not something the mind could fix. Some very basic structures within my personality had to be altered. This could only happen, I believe, with the help of a skilled therapist. I was lucky that Carl was there when I needed him.

An Easter Morning Trip to the Emergency Room

Even as I am learning to deal with symptoms more realistically, sharp pains in my chest or dull aches in the stomach invariably make me think, Is this it? Is my life over? I feel somewhat calm, but still I have a heightened awareness of the next few minutes, waiting, listening to my body. Is the pain gone? Will it come back?

On April 19, 1987, Easter Sunday, I awoke with a dull pain in the upper abdomen, just below the diaphragm. It felt like the pain I had had with my heart attack. And it was in the same location. I took an antacid and waited, afraid to get out of bed. I told Judy how I was feeling and we waited fifteen minutes for the antacid to work. I prayed. I cursed my luck. I was so tired of feeling myself in danger. I wasn't imagining it. The pain was real, persistent.

"We should go to the emergency room," Judy said.

"I don't want to go," I said. My tears were sparse and bitter.

We waited a few more minutes and when the pain did not abate, I got dressed and we drove to the emergency room of the nearest hospital. I brought with me my medical records. The physician on duty did a clinical examination and then an EKG. I was put on an IV, blood was taken for the enzyme tests.

The EKG showed a myocardial infarction, but the readout of an EKG cannot distinguish between an historical infarction and one in process. More waiting for the laboratory blood results. And finally—several hours later—the doctor's opinion. The pain was caused by acute gastrointestinal distress. Perhaps an infection or something I had eaten. The night before, we had eaten at an Indian restaurant, and I had consumed a small plate of onions. That could have done it. After four hours in the emergency room, I was released. I went home feeling a mixture of strong emotions: jubilant, relieved, angry, and sad.

Turning points. As I've noted, my early experience as a heart attack victim (although I don't particularly like the word *victim*, it's apt, because that's how I felt) was that my life had changed dramatically and that I would never be the same again. This meant, I assumed, I would never take long trips, especially to those places that didn't have modern medical facilities. I would never engage in robust activities like skiing. These assumptions were not thought out so much as felt. I was eventually able to reverse this invalid psychology by making reasoned judgments about what I was capable of doing and then acting.

Several examples stand out. In January 1987, right after my consultation with Dr. Bodnar, Judy and I were invited to St. Maarten for a Caribbean vacation by my sister Erika and her husband. They had been given the use of a villa for a week. It came as a revelation to me, on a feeling level, that I could take long swims in the ocean, that I could snorkel, that I could dance. We went to a nightclub one night where I danced, fast and feverish, with Judy, my sister, and even a stranger, a young attractive singer. At Orient Beach, where bathing suits were optional, I swam naked. I felt no inhibitions striding down the beach to the snack bar. I had lost ten pounds after my heart attack and still hadn't gained it back. Even though I was the thinnest person on the beach, even though the bones in my shoulders protruded, I felt *good* about my body. I didn't care how it looked to other people. It was my body, by God. It had gone through bad times, but it had survived. No matter how it looked it deserved to be celebrated. Trouncing barebottomed down the beach I felt as if I were a Masai warrior. Proud and regal and beautiful.

I did not ski that first winter—my first cardiologist had advised against it. The cold weather, he cautioned, together with the sporadic nature of the exercise, might not be good for my heart. The following winter David Putnam said there was no reason I shouldn't ski. Still I felt reluctant. Why take a chance? Because of the beauty, Judy reminded me. Looking down at the snow-clad mountains from the chairlift. The lovely feeling of swishing down the trails. With her gentle prodding I finally agreed to go. It was even more exhilarating than

I remembered. The startling snowscapes. The silence. The tranquility. The two of us being together as we had been before. The body's natural rhythm as it floats and sways, gliding down the mountain. Occasionally an unwelcome thought would pop into my head: "What if I have a pain? What if? What if?" And I'd reply, "No. I'm fine. See what my body can do, how strong it is. I'm fine. I'm fine. I'm fine."

Body Proud

The skiing, like the swimming and the snorkeling and the dancing, seemed miraculous. I no longer felt as if I were an invalid. My body spoke proudly, like a child. "See me. Look what I can do."

In January 1988 I had to go in for my annual thallium stress test. A few months before the examination I once again went into training. I thought of the test as a friendly competition with myself. Last January I had entered Stage Four of the Bruce Protocol. This year could I get to Stage Five?

On the day of the test, it was snowing heavily. In the examination room were my cardiologist, Dr. Putnam, a radiologist who would inject the thallium into the IV, and several nurses who would monitor my blood pressure and work the treadmill. Dr. Putnam had given me the usual instructions. I was to tell him when I was really tired and wanted to quit, and he would direct that the thallium be injected. I would then have to exercise for another twenty seconds in order for the thallium to be absorbed. In retrospect I realize my attitude was probably not the best. I was determined not to admit I was tired. I had asked David Putnam to let me know when I entered Stage Four. When he signaled me, I was huffing but still had plenty of energy in reserve. And then, in keeping with a crazy and admittedly macho plan, I told the group a joke.

"A couple in their eighties, widow and widower, met in their retirement community in Florida and fell in love. They decided to get married." Puff, puff. "On their wedding night, Mr. Thomas is waiting in bed for his bride to come out of the bathroom." Puff, puff,

puff. "She finally emerges. Standing against the wall, she lets her nightgown fall from her body." Puff! Gasp! Gasp! Puff!

"You've just entered Stage Five," says Dr. Putnam.

"I'm not done with the joke," I reply. "'Dear, there's something I got to tell you,' she says. 'I've got acute angina.'"

"We're injecting the thallium," says Dr. Putnam. "You've done terrific."

"Right." Twenty more seconds, I tell myself. Don't fall on your face. "And Mr. Thomas says, 'I hope so, because you sure have lousy tits.'"

CHAPTER 23

Survivor's Debt

My one business preoccupation in the months following my heart attack was the plaza I was developing for charity. I had put a great deal of effort into leasing the seven stores that would comprise the center. I had contacted real-estate brokers, placed advertisements in the newspaper, and had written or called numerous retail chains as well as individual stores. Were they thinking about expansion? Were they looking for new sites? If I got a yes, I would try to convince the real-estate representative or owner that the Whittler Plaza was an ideal location. I described what it would look like: an L-shaped modern building with plenty of windows for display and individualized storefronts in tile or marble; green canopies around the front of the building that would be lit at night, giving off a luminescent glow. And the sculpture by E. Seward Johnson, Jr., the centerpiece of the plaza, The Whittler—a lifelike, life-size young man, wearing a blue sweater, sitting on a bench where he whittled with a small knife.

I signed up one tenant right away, and then a second. After that, for a long time, nothing happened. I had tried everything but prayer.

I Believed in God in My Heart

The God I believed in was an amorphous Everything, an Energy, an Intelligence that did not, that by Its Nature *could* not, interfere in the lives of men. It was certainly not the personal God of the Judeo-Christian tradition who could listen to the nearly 5 billion souls upon the earth, and who would occasionally grant their petitions. And yet I found myself thinking every now and then, "C'mon, God, after all it's really *Your* plaza. It's to help your people, the ones in need. I'm doing my share. Would you just help me a bit?" And even more strange—for me, at least—I had faith that He would help. Building a plaza on speculation, that is, before it's at least 50 percent preleased, is risky. But I took the risk, knowing that He would make it work. Not bad, considering I really didn't believe. In retrospect I suppose it's more accurate to say I believed in my heart but not in my head.

By November 1986 the plaza was complete and 70 percent leased; there would be enough money to pay the expenses and the mortgage. I scheduled an official opening early in December. The opening would also serve as a fund-raiser for a local charity, the Northeast Regional Food Bank, which collects and distributes food to soup kitchens and pantries in twenty-one upstate counties. I had read about the organization and chose it as our first recipient because it seemed so effective in helping the hungry. For every one dollar contributed, the organization was able to collect and distribute thirteen dollars in food.

I asked those who benefited financially from the project to make contributions and many of them did: the general contractor, architect, several subcontractors, the former owners of the property, and the bank. Altogether over $13,000 was raised, the lion's share coming from the plaza owners.

I wrote a dedication for the plaza and had it inscribed on three small plaques, one for the building and the others for the people I called "co-inspirators"—Paul Newman and A. E. Hotchner and Governor Mario Cuomo, whose theme-of-family speech at the Democratic National Convention of 1984 had moved me deeply.

I asked a friend, a county legislator, to host the ceremony. My father read the dedication. Our building manager presented the $13,000 to the executive director of the food bank. I sat in the back of the room with the other invited guests, comfortable with my anonymity. I believed then—I obviously no longer do—that our good deeds should be kept secret. It would be shameful—would it not?—to seek acknowledgment or praise. No, let my father have the limelight (who taught me that?). Let the people come up to him and pat him on the back. What a fine job you did! How well you spoke! I was a good son. I had learned my lessons well.

In the months that followed I began to wonder about my motivation. Why had I really built the plaza? Didn't I secretly crave some acknowledgment, a little praise? Of course I did. Why else had I sent the plaques to Newman and Hotchner and to Governor Cuomo? What else would account for those occasional fantasies I would find myself entertaining: "Hello, David, this is Paul Newman. I called to say you did a nice thing." Or: "This is Mario Cuomo and I called to thank you for your kind words in the dedication." They didn't call. I really didn't expect they would. Yet I was a little disappointed.

But seeking praise from famous father-figures was only a piece of it, a small piece. I recalled my obsession. For years I had thought about doing something significant for charity. No idle daydream, this was something I *had* to do. I would find no peace until I did.

Understanding the Obsession

In April, my friend Vera Fryling came from California to visit for a week. We had many good talks—we always do—and in one of them I spoke of my obsession and its fruition. After hearing my story, she smiled in that easy way of hers. "That I can understand," she said. "Survivor's debt." As soon as she uttered the words, I knew her analysis was correct.

The next day I went to my study and in one sitting typed a small essay using Vera's words as the title, "Survivor's Debt." In it I talked about my obsession, about Newman and Hotchner, about the plaza, and about my inability to understand what was driving me until Vera said the words. Vera understood not only because she was a psychiatrist who knew me well, but because she, too, was a survivor. A young Jewish woman raised in Berlin in the 1930s, her family killed by the Nazis, she and her mother managed to survive by fleeing their home and changing their identities. After the war she emigrated to

America and became a psychiatrist. When breast cancer was diagnosed, she was told by her physicians not to bother to finish her residency. But she did and she beat the disease. In 1979 she was shot three times in the stomach on the streets of San Francisco by a hoodlum who wanted her car. He had tried to finish her off by driving over her, but she was able to roll out of the way. Vera knew about survival.

In my article I reflected upon how much, after being cured of Hodgkin's, I wanted to make my life count, as if making my life count, making a significant contribution, would keep me alive. Although I never spoke to God, I seemed to be saying to Him, in my unacknowledged faith of the heart, "God, I know you don't make bargains, but please consider me worthy to live out a normal life. Look what I am willing to do. The money the plaza should generate for charity is just the beginning. Keep me around. You'll see I'm worth it."

I ended the essay by mentioning my heart attack and my unspoken words to God. "After all," I might now say to the God I never speak to and who I don't acknowledge exists, "I built the plaza. What more do you want? Although we never struck a bargain—in fact never even spoke about it—I assumed You would watch over me."

And God replies: "I did. You survived, didn't you? You're still here. What more do *you* want?"

I concluded: Now I have to wonder, What more do I owe? What else must I do to stay alive?

I mailed the article to the "About Men" column of the *New York Times Magazine* and it was accepted. It appeared in the August 30, 1987, issue, just eight days after the anniversary of my heart attack. It was thrilling to see my thoughts in print. It was also the beginning of my being able to speak openly of who I was and who I am. The letters I received in response to the article were from people who, like myself, had survived in some way or another—an illness, the loss of a loved one, alcoholism, drug abuse. They, too, felt they owed a debt. A nun wrote, praising me for my charitable work, and several evangelicals wrote long letters explaining that if I believed in Jesus I would be saved; I wouldn't have to do anything. One even sent me a Bible. A family member had criticized me for suggesting publicly that I did not believe in God. A priest wrote, pointing out that God expressed Himself through people and thanking me for participating in His work.

Barn Raisers: A Simple Idea That Worked

I no longer felt, as I had when I wrote the article, that I must continue to do good works to stay alive. But a month after the article appeared, I began to have thoughts of another charitable venture. I discussed it with Judy.

"Are you sure you want to do that?" she asked. "It sounds like a lot of work. And you said you wanted to focus on your writing."

That was true. Because I had limited amounts of energy, I had decided to wear only one hat: writer. At least for the time being. But my charitable idea seemed like such a good one. I decided to make it a reality.

The idea was very simple. Instead of asking people to contribute money to yet another charity, ask them to give their services or discount the cost of their products on cooperative charitable ventures. The not-for-profit organization that would facilitate this process would be called Barn Raisers.

I called my brother and told him about it. Would he help me form the organization? His response was immediate: "Tell me what you want me to do." I suggested that we donate a commercial lot that we owned to Barn Raisers. Then we would enlist a team of people—architects, contractors, bankers, lawyers—to erect a building on a reduced-cost basis. We would lease or sell the building and give all the money to charity. Part of the money would go to hire a part-time director for Barn Raisers. His or her function would be to assess the construction and repair needs of local charitable organizations and to coordinate future projects. "Do I have the lot?" I asked my brother. "You've got it," he replied.

The nice thing about what I thought of as my simple idea was that it worked. I wrote letters and then called about fifty businesspeople to ask them to lend their names to the organization. I emphasized that joining did not require a commitment to do anything. It merely meant they agreed with the goals of the organization and would consider participating in projects sponsored by Barn Raisers. Nearly all of the people I called agreed to become members.

The people I asked to contribute to our first project agreed to discount their services from 25 to 50 percent. And one friend, Joe Clark, who owns a construction company, agreed to serve as general contractor without any fee at all.

Then something serendipitous happened. A real-estate broker telephoned to ask if the lot my brother and I planned to donate was for sale. The Heart Association needed a new headquarters and the lot was located right where they wanted to be. Suddenly the Barn Raisers project to raise money for charity became the Barn Raisers project to erect a new Heart Association building. As I write this, the building is under construction. The cost of the 7,800-square-foot building to the Heart Association will be $480,000, which is $300,000 less than the present market value of $780,000 for a similar building in that area.

Barn Raisers is probably, in part, continued payment of my survivor's debt. But I don't feel compelled to continue its work; it is not an obsession. Rather, my involvement stems from a very clear awareness that our world is in pretty bad shape and that some people are in desperate need of bare essentials—food, clothing, shelter, medical and psychological services. I know that government will not and apparently cannot adequately supply these needs. And so it becomes obvious to me that those of us who can afford to give—money, material goods, services, or perhaps most important our time, our presence, our loving concern—should do so.

In Search of a Personal God

And what about God? Where does He enter in all of this? One of the few books I read in the first year following my heart attack was William James's *Varieties of Religious Experience*. Reading it convinced me of what I already deeply felt: that one is much better off believing in a personal God than not. Or better yet, not simply believing, but *knowing*. When Carl Jung was asked whether he believed in God, he said, "No, I don't believe. I know."

I wish I could walk back into the Catholic church and find God waiting for me there. But the authoritarianism and the patriarchy of the Church offends me. I wish I could speak with God, not when I'm in desperate need, but in easy conversation, the conversation I would have with a friend who I know loves me and wishes me well. I would like to find God, not simply because I would feel better believing, but because He exists and because friendship with our God, our Creator, our co-Creator, whatever our relationship, is the natural order of things.

But finding God is not easy. His (or Her) terms for relationship appear onerous. Friendship, human friendship, I tell myself, friendship which I so highly value, takes time, does it not? And commitment. Loving presence. Trust. These qualities must be freely given to God, I would suspect, if He is to reveal Himself. But He won't reveal Himself unless I believe, I say. How am I to believe?

In order to believe in God, I must first believe in God.

Well, there it is. I am a monkey with my tail tied to my nose, chasing myself around a tree.

I am sitting hunched over my typewriter in Chris's room, looking out the window. Samantha lies asleep on the bed. I don't like endings, and so I think of this moment as a beginning. Let's see. The first thing I must do is untie my tail from my nose. Then stand away from the tree, for the tree blocks my view. Now I must sniff the air and set out in a promising direction. Or sit here and wait. Either choice seems pregnant with possibilities.

CHAPTER 24

Looking Back

W hen I recalled my conversations with Dr. S, the psychiatric resident with Hodgkin's whom I had met at Yale–New Haven Hospital, I realized that before I finished my story I would have to find out what happened to him. I knew that his liver biopsy had turned out negative, and he had tolerated the full dose of treatment. Judy and I went to his apartment for dinner before he and his wife and son left Albany. I had thought of him, from time to time, throughout the past twenty years. I had assumed, had hoped, he had survived. The last time I saw him was in the fall of 1969.

I put off making the inquiry about Dr. S as long as I could. A few days ago I learned that his disease recurred in 1973 and he died in 1975. I was shocked and saddened. It is still difficult for me to believe. He was a hardy, good-humored man who loved his wife and child. I mourn his passing.

Walking Into the Future; Looking at the Past

At this moment I am walking slowly into my future, for I am in no hurry to reach the finish line. My head is cast back, looking over my shoulder at the near distance, the middle, and the far. I want to tell you what I see.

In the far distance, I see a young man who is tall, a little over six foot, and thin, weighing about 140 pounds. He is in love with a young woman named Judy and she loves him in return. He is ambitious and confident—he intends to be both a writer and a psychotherapist—and yet he is afraid to tell his father what he wants to do with his life. She finds that strange. She also finds his strong desire to be a father unusual. He's only twenty-one and the young men she has met have never talked about fathering the way he has.

When he finally reveals the secrets of his life-goals to his father—a moment painful for both of them—the young man has taken a significant step toward independence. But when he withdraws from the graduate program in psychology because he finds the stress-induced physical symptoms he's been suffering unbearable, he steps back into dependency.

The self-loathing caused by his failure affects his immune system and makes him more susceptible to physical illness. He attends law school, as his father wished, knowing in his heart he is betraying himself. Nevertheless he does well—he *achieves*, for that is his nature—but within two years of graduation he is diagnosed with Hodgkin's disease. He feels terrified, devastated . . . and ashamed. He insists his illness be kept a secret. For the next two years, he lives a life of dread, fearing, despite the excellent treatment he has received and a favorable prognosis, that the disease will recur. It does.

And in the middle distance I see myself in my early thirties sparked by the words of hope from some higher source. *Know that you are well and you will find the means of survival.* I search my soul and come to realize that I was in part responsible for becoming ill. The self-hatred, the self-betrayal, the diminution of my will to live, the surrender of my dreams . . . I might as well have drunk poison. Although I feel responsible, I do not blame myself for becoming ill, for there was no willfulness, no understanding of the link between negative messages of the mind and their pernicious effect on the emotions and the body.

Silva Mind Control taught me meditation and visualization techniques to enhance my healing. These practices are important in prevention as well as cure, and so I still use them today.

I applied the Edgar Cayce remedies for Hodgkin's for over three years. Although I don't use Cayce's remedies anymore, I am still influenced by his ideas, particularly his emphasis on balance and the importance of maintaining a positive attitude about oneself and one's life. I have never taken this to mean that one's fear, sadness, or anger should be ignored or repressed. I believe the opposite is true. These feelings should be experienced deeply and fully, perhaps with the help of a skilled therapist. It is only through the acknowledgment and experience of our emotions that we will be able to assimilate them so they may have an appropriate, but not undue effect on our lives. Judy and I have seldom discussed my illness and the feelings it generated for both of us. Since I began writing this account, which she has read, we began to talk about that period in our lives. She remembered feeling emotionally abandoned, and her recollection, even after all these years, carried an emotional charge. Sadness. Anger. Listening to her describe the pain she had endured made me sad, too. These conversations weren't pleasant, but they were natural and authentic and, I believe, necessary.

I was fortunate in finding an acupuncturist as skilled as Dr. Siow. I know my body changed after his initial treatments, and I suspect acupuncture was a significant factor in my getting well. I've sent family and friends to Dr. Siow, and all of them were helped for various conditions, including allergies, arthritis, and migraine.

I was also fortunate that Olga Worrall came into my life. Only God knows for sure whether the laying on of hands I received from her "charged my batteries," as she would say, bolstering my immune system so that a cure was more likely. But something happened that day in Baltimore when she touched me and I felt the hot, tingling energy move up my spine.

I am still a strong believer that faith healing can and sometimes does result in miracles. When we were living in California, Judy was rushed to the hospital with severe pain caused by an ovarian cyst which had become infected. She was quite sick for over a week. One of the things I did was call Olga Worrall, who agreed to do absent healing. And when Judy was able to leave the hospital, I arranged for a local healer to administer the laying on of hands.

Each year more and more books are published about the mind-body connection and the importance of attitude and the will to live in the healing process. Whether it is a personal story like my own or scientific studies or theoretical explanations, the information adds, I believe, to a growing collective consciousness that the mind can have a significant role in the restoration of health. Some physicians, generally referred to as holistic, consciously enlist the patient's entire being—body, emotions, mind, and spirit—into a strategy for healing. In the future no physician will think to do otherwise. More and more people are seeking to share the responsibility for their wellness. They are more aware that certain lifestyles (e.g., a fast-lane life that you don't *enjoy*) or intolerable situations (staying in a dead marriage is one) can literally make you sick.

Becoming a New Being

Still in the middle distance, I see myself not merely doing the things I was supposed to do—whether meditation, Cayce treatments, or reading inspirational books—but *changing*. The episode at the lake of losing my selves, which I experienced as a snakelike shedding of dead skin, was transformative. In that frightening and mysterious moment, I died and was reborn. Joseph Campbell tells us that the snake, in Eastern traditions, is the symbol of new life. The lake experience was also a symbol, a precursor of what was to come. I remember the enormous clarity I had in the days following that experience. I thought: I can no longer be who I was. It's not simply a matter of changing. I must become a new person, a new being.

Witnessing the communication with the dead at that Spiritualist church. The prophecy that I would meet a teacher. "Seeing" my Inca spirit guide. Receiving the laying on of hands. Out-of-body experiences. Lucid dreams. Watching the rainbow cloud pass over the head of the boy guru, the Mararaj-ji. These and other experiences expanded my personal boundaries. I was not a grander or better person, but I had an increased capacity for different, more complex experiences. Impossible dreams became realistic goals. I *could* become a psychotherapist. I *could* become a stand-up comic. The old David Tate was still inside of me somewhere. I had retained that old software, if you will. But now I had access to a seemingly limitless supply of new programs that I could help create. My personhood was not simply the result of my past but was a continual act of co-creation.

Co-creation? Who is the co-creator? God, of course. Or call it something else. Higher Self, Cosmic Consciousness, Supreme Intelligence. It doesn't matter, for as the Hindus point out, God is beyond all names and forms.

Whatever else God is, God is Life. She sustains my very existence just as She sustains the existence of a flower or a flea. Unless God continues to create me both in time and in eternity, I will cease to be.

While I am speaking of God, of whom I know not a whisper, I am aware that he is not my father. I have often, I realize, confused the two in my mind and heart. Angry father, angry God. Punitive father, punitive God. I must please my father. I must please God. The confusion is natural. In Judeo-Christian tradition, we are taught to think of ourselves as God's children. I think the metaphor is unfortunate. God is often given a bum rap. On the other hand, the confusion sometimes works to God's advantage. I have a close friend, a Dominican priest, who has a profound faith in a God whose unconditional love for His creatures is powerful and poignant. I once asked my friend about his parents. His loving description allowed me to understand why his God is so benevolent and kind.

In the near distance I see a middle-aged man who appears to be balding! I often catch him looking out at me from the bathroom mirror, and though I am sometimes shocked by the sight of his brown-gray beard, and the lines which clearly show his age, I try not to show it. (Hahahanda tells his audiences, "If you think this is baldness"— pointing to his forehead, which is so high it has no ceiling—"you are mistaken. No, you see, one day I awoke with the intuition that very soon my third eye would open. What you see is not baldness, but a landing strip I have created for my third eye.")

Two and a half years ago this man, who despite his forty-eight years looks fairly healthy, had a heart attack. I know it seems hard to believe, but his doctors confirm it is true. And he believes it. He remembers his terror. For a moment he thought he was dying. When he returned from the hospital and was out of danger, you would think he'd have bounced back. He bounced like putty. He had the energy of an old man—no less! His eighty-eight-year-old father could run circles around him. And he had fears of a child.

What could he do? Nothing. *Stop doing.* He finally came to that wisdom and was content to just look out the window. No planning or rehearsing, but *seeing*. He loosened the reins on himself and his life. He let the horse pull the cart and he sat back and enjoyed the ride.

He knew, of course, that there were certain things he had to do. Aerobic exercise was no longer optional but mandatory (for he did suffer a heart attack). He lowered his cholesterol and meditated, visualizing the blood flowing freely through the wide arteries of his heart. He went to a psychiatrist so that mending from this fresh trauma would make him stronger than he had been before.

Then one morning he awoke. A force propelled him from his bed to his typewriter. He began to write the story of his healing. Like so many other things he had done, so many things that seemed inevitable and right, he felt as if the idea was not his own. He was compelled to write just as he had been compelled to build the plaza for charity. He had been given a suggestion which he understood was an opportunity. Without any thought or analysis he accepted it with a fierce enthusiasm.

Revealing Myself Was Another Step in My Healing Journey

I didn't realize until I was finished that writing my story, telling you who I was and am, was yet another step on my healing journey. I think of all the secrets I've kept, as defenses against rejection or shame or ridicule. My mother's illness. My desire to become a psychotherapist. My illness. My decision to leave law and move to California to study transpersonal psychology. My involvement in charity. So many secrets.

I've come to believe that each time I revealed myself, I became healthier. The big secrets which I carried were like lead stones. But every pretense, every lie, white or black, every subterfuge was a needless weight on my body. Even the masks of social convention now seem too heavy to bear.

I am lighter now.

About the Author

A man of wide-ranging abilities, with professional expertise in several key areas, David A. Tate has worked as a psychotherapist, real estate developer, writer, comic, and, on occasion, in his original profession, as a lawyer. Since his recovery from a heart attack, he has focused on writing, and on a new venture, Barn Raisers, a non-profit organization he founded to help other charitable organizations with their repair and building needs.

Tate, who lives with his wife and family in upstate New York, realized a life-long dream when, more than ten years ago, he first performed as a stand-up comic in a San Francisco comedy club. Since that time, he has developed a character, Hahahanda, who tells his audiences about his manic search to find a guru.

Tate is a graduate of Fordham University and the Albany Law School. He received his M.A. degree in clinical psychology from John F. Kennedy University in Orinda, California. As a psychotherapist, he has worked with individuals, couples, and juvenile sex offenders.